IT'S OUR ASSEMBLY

Assembly topics for 5-8s

ANNE FARNCOMBE

NATIONAL CHRISTIAN EDUCATION COUNCIL

Robert Denholm House
Nutfield, Redhill, Surrey, RH1 4HW

To EILEEN and CHRIS

First published 1979
© Anne Farncombe

0 7197 0220 8

Typeset by Surrey Graphics Ltd, Dorking, Surrey
Printed and bound by W & J Mackay Ltd, Chatham, Kent

Contents

Introduction

This book is published in response to a need expressed by many teachers for material for assemblies and, in particular, material which is linked to class-room projects.

All the necessary material for assemblies is provided here including stories, poems, hymns and prayers, based on a variety of topics following through the terms of the school year.

The projects are written in outline form, and give sufficient indication both of the way in which the projects can be set up in the class-room and of how the resultant work of the children can be used within the assembly.

Throughout the book, for ease of presentation only, teachers are referred to as *she*; similarly the words *Infant school* and *Infants* have been used to indicate both Infant and First schools, and the children in them. The hymns and songs have been selected from two books commonly used in Infant and First schools: *New Child Songs* (NCEC) and *Someone's Singing, Lord* (A & C Black Ltd).

Anne Farncombe is a trained teacher with many years' experience in various schools. She is married to a Chief Inspector of the NSPCC and they have five children, all adopted.

New things

Project outline

This theme is designed to be used at the beginning of a term, and most appropriately at the beginning of the new school year in September. Many class teachers will find very little time for concentrating their attention on planning an assembly service at this time. But, as each child gets to know his or her new teacher and, in reception classes, his or her new classmates, it will be quite a simple matter for the teacher to connect the theme of this assembly with the work of the week.

Knowing that an assembly is coming, the teacher will need to bring this 'newness' to the attention of the class quite often in conversation: 'John has found the new game of Ludo; it was ordered specially for you when Miss Pitts said I could buy some new toys', or 'We have to get to the playground by a new door now that we are in this classroom', or 'Let's learn some new words today' and so on. Talk together about new things and looking after them, new birthday toys, new clothes, new books, new pencils.

Make a display of new work, showing new skills, or the use of new materials. Try new physical activity, such as a dance, or difficult, more advanced work on PE apparatus. New clothes, especially new school clothes, should be admired, drawn and, depending on the age of the children, written about. Probably during the week a new song will be sung or a poem learnt, and these could be practised with the assembly in mind. If a 'junk box' is already in the class-room, some children might like to make something new from something old.

Many members of the class will have brothers and sisters who will also be going to new classes or schools, and so this theme will be one which naturally spills over into the home. The teacher should be quick to make use of any 'new' situations arising out of the children's news — father's new job, a new house, a new neighbour, a new baby or new toys. Such items could be recorded in pictures and words to be displayed or read at the assembly.

If there is time, holiday news could be followed up, news of new places visited, new experiences of travelling, eating, and listening to new languages; new friends on the beach, coach, or in a hotel or holiday camp, could be drawn, talked and written about.

At the assembly, new children to the class or school should be specially mentioned and welcomed and, particularly if they have come from abroad, it should be pointed out how strange and perhaps frightening this 'newness' can be. Talk to the class about this before the assembly, if possible, and try to elicit from them ideas on how to make things happier and easier for such children.

The assembly

Hymns and songs

What makes the day-time after every night?	NCS 20	
Father, we thank you for the night	NCS 32	SSL1
When Jesus was a little boy	NCS 57	
Stand up, clap hands, shout thank you, Lord	SSL 14	

Poem

My mother took me to the school
When I was old enough.
The older children frightened me —
They looked so big and rough.
I didn't want my Mum to go —
I very nearly cried;
The teacher said, 'Here, hold my hand
And keep close by my side.'
I looked at books, I drank my milk,
I sang a nursery rhyme,
I played with lots and lots of toys —
I had a lovely time.
When Mummy came to take me home
I nearly cried once more;
This time I didn't want to leave
When she took me to the door!
'I'm coming back right after lunch
To play some more with you,'
I shouted as I left the room —
To John, 'cos he was new.
Being new is not so bad;
I thought it was at first,

But when you've played and made a friend
You're over all the worst.

Music
    Chanson de Matin, Elgar
    Morning from *Peer Gynt Suite,* Grieg

Prayer
    O God, we are finding so many new things; we are doing so many new things; help us to be happy and to make other people happy, too.

Stories
    Bible story: Looking after the new baby — Exodus 2.1-10
    Caring for new things (told in full)

Caring for new things

It was David's birthday. He arrived at school carrying a large paper bag containing a funnily-shaped object. 'It's my new robot,' he told his friends in the playground. 'My Dad and Mum gave it to me for my birthday. Dad said I could bring it to school just to show everybody. But I'm not to play with it out in the playground. It might break.'

Miss Baron was careful with the robot. She wouldn't let the other boys and girls hold it, even when they asked very politely, but she told David he could show them how it worked. Clearing a space, David wound up the robot with a key, and everyone watched as it strutted across the floor. It hissed and spat coloured sparks, and looked this way and that as it went. It was very smart, very shiny, very new. It was better than any of David's other toys, and he wanted it to last for ever.

That night the robot was wrapped in tissue paper so that it wouldn't get scratched, and put back into its box. 'I'm going to look after my new toy really well,' David told his mother, 'so that it will last a long, long time.'

A few days later David had another surprise. A huge green van drew up outside the empty house next door, and some men began unpacking furniture. A new family was moving in at last! Later in the day David saw a boy kicking a ball about in the garden next door. 'Hello,' he shouted through a gap in the fence.

The other boy looked up and came over to the gap. 'What's your name?' he asked, and David told him. 'I'm Mark Johnson,' said the boy, 'and I'm eight.'

'Do you want to see my robot?' asked David, pleased to have found a new friend. He carried it out carefully to the gap in the fence. Mark thought the robot was wonderful and wanted to wind it up himself. David was doubtful, but he liked his new friend and allowed him to wind up the robot. Mark crawled through the gap and they both watched as the robot marched away along the garden path. They played together until it was time for tea.

'I've got a new friend,' David told his mother as he wrapped his robot up again for the night; he was taking great care of it. 'We're going to play football tomorrow after school, and he's asked me to show him where the library is.'

But the next evening David had forgotten his promise. Another friend, Peter, called and together they went off to play at Peter's house. They played with the robot on the garden path, and then they climbed a tree, and then they went indoors for some chocolate biscuits. Peter lent David his new police car, and David said he'd take care of it. He didn't see Peter again until after school on Monday, three days later, and he hadn't seen his new friend Mark since that first afternoon together.

'Hey, David,' said Peter, 'did you know you left your new robot in my garden last Friday? Mum found it this morning. It's gone a bit rusty because it was left out in the wet.'

David looked at it in horror — his new, shiny robot! He had forgotten all about it! Now it was dull, and it felt rough, and it squeaked. He almost cried. Mother said he should have looked after it.

David called over the fence, 'Is Mark there?' he asked Mrs Johnson, who was gardening.

'No; he's waited for you each evening,' she said. 'Now he's gone off to the park by himself.'

David went indoors sadly. It was all going wrong: his new toy was spoiled — he might be able to clean it up and oil it, but it would never be so shiny-new again. And now his new friend had deserted him.

'You had a new robot, and you knew that it wouldn't go on working properly if you didn't look after it,' said his mother. 'You had a new friend too. You have to look after new friends as well as new toys, you know. Friendship doesn't work properly if you don't look after it.'

Suddenly, being friends with Mark next door seemed more important than the new robot. David began to run down the road to the park. 'Hi, Mark!' he was shouting. 'I'm coming! We'll play football, I promise!'

Our hands

Project outline

A project on hands is worth doing at any time of the year, and can be as long or as short as the teacher wishes to make it. It can lead into any subject, or be limited to 'hand' work. The thought behind it, if it is to lead up to a meaningful assembly, should be that hands are God's tools, and that what we make or fashion with them can reflect our ideas of God, and that the way in which we use them in our dealings with each other conveys much of what we are like as people.

Even the smallest children — perhaps especially the smallest children — are aware of their hands, as they feel and fashion, trying to co-ordinate their minds and movements.

At the end of a day when the children have been actively engaged in making, modelling and drawing for much of the time, the teacher should conclude the afternoon by asking what things the children have used most. Some will say pencils, or paper, or scissors; most will need to be led to think about the tools (their hands) that have done much of the work. Some of the work accomplished should be mounted as examples of this, and displayed ready for the assembly.

If the children are at a suitable stage, hands make excellent simple measuring instruments, eg, how many hand-spans go across the table top, or black-board, or door? Hands can be drawn round and cut out. Further measuring can then be done with these 'rulers'. They can be used as comparative symbols, eg, bigger than, smaller than; or 'John's is the biggest hand, whose is the smallest?' and so on.

Attractively coloured and decorated paper hands, joined together at the bases with paper clips or staples, make excellent 'floral' displays for the class-room or presents for home, especially when attached to a thin rod for a stalk. When coloured yellow, and stuck with the fingers pointing outward in a large circle, they can become a large 'sun'. If time allows, the children would enjoy making finger and palm prints, which can be used as patterns, or simply for comparison one with another.

There should be as much discussion as possible about what hands can do, eg, knitting and needlework, model-making, pottery, cooking; they are

9

necessary for riding a bicycle, for eating, for climbing trees or PE apparatus, for playing cricket or doing jig-saw puzzles. The list is endless. Each child could write about or draw some activity that involves using hands.

Hands are also used to convey feelings or messages. Talk a little about finger language for the deaf, or braille for the blind. A smack or slap conveys a quick message, experienced by many of the children! A hug, on the other hand, gives a feeling of warmth and love; a handshake is given in greeting. The children will know the feeling of security and protection given by an adult as they walk hand-in-hand along the street, or as the child is guided into some new situation.

A whole section of activities involving the use of hands to feel with could be included, and the teacher will develop and add to what is suggested here. A range of textures, shapes and sizes could be explored by the hands and recorded; and guessing games of discovery by touch played.

For the assembly, some of the work done during the preparation time can be used and talked about; hand games or rhymes can be shared, and activities involving hand movement shown (such as making a 'cat's cradle' or playing a 'pat-a-cake' game). Perhaps the teacher has recently seen hands being used in the wrong way in the class-room or playground — for hitting, squeezing, pulling, pinching or pushing. Talk about this at the assembly; then emphasise the good things that hands can do: helping, guiding, soothing, etc. Putting hands together (to capture straying thoughts) for prayer could lead naturally into the moment when the children talk to God.

The assembly

Hymns and songs

Babies are tiny — their hands are quite small	NCS 98
Hands to work and feet to run	SSL 21
It fell upon a summer day	SSL 31
Jesus' hands were kind hands	SSL 33

Poem

Jesus' hands were used a lot,
To help and heal and show the way;
They had great strength,
They had great warmth,
They worked hard every day.

May my hands be strong hands, too,
And may they loving be,
That every day someone may say
They see God's love in me.

Prayer

Thank you, dear God, for our hands and what we can do with them. Help us always to use them to be kind and helpful.

Stories

Bible stories: The kind hands of Jesus: Simon Peter's mother-in-law —
                    Mark 1.29-31
                    The two blind men — Matthew 20.29-34
                    The children come to Jesus — Mark 10.13-16 (told in full)

The children come to Jesus

When Hannah and John were old enough they were allowed to climb the hills outside their village. It was on one of these walks that they first saw Jesus. He noticed them playing together and smiled as he passed. He often went that way, and always he smiled, and sometimes he waved. Usually there were people with him, his own special friends and men and women from the nearby villages.

One day lots of people followed Jesus over the hills: people from their own village, neighbours and relatives. John and Hannah watched them go. A little later John said, 'I want to go as well. Come on, Hannah, let's go and find Jesus.'

'We must ask Mother first,' said Hannah sensibly. 'Perhaps she'll come as well.'

They ran home. 'Mother,' called Hannah as she went inside the house. It was dark after being out in the bright sunshine. 'Come up to the hills with us. John and I want to see Jesus, and we know he's up there somewhere.'

'Can we go, Mother, can we go?' asked John, tugging at Mother's hand.

'It's getting late,' said Mother. 'The other people will be coming home soon. Jesus will be tired. He won't want us rushing up to see him now.'

'Yes, he will, I know he will!' John said. He ran out and began to scramble up the path between the houses.

Mother followed more slowly with Hannah. Many people were already coming down, talking and smiling as they came. Sometimes Hannah caught the word 'Jesus', and she knew that these men and women had been with him. Perhaps he would have moved away. Perhaps he would be resting.

11

Perhaps ...

'Come on, Mother, hurry!' she urged.

Higher up the hill some more people were coming down. 'I couldn't see him,' said one little girl. 'We couldn't get near enough.'

'Come with us,' said Mother. 'Perhaps if we go now Jesus will be able to talk to you.'

Another mother with two children hesitated. 'We'll go back as well,' she said, and they all turned round to climb back up the hill. The younger children ran off shouting, 'Jesus! Jesus! We want to see Jesus!' The other children, including John and Hannah, began racing across the grass to where Jesus was sitting.

Suddenly a man stood in front of them. 'Be quiet!' he ordered. 'Jesus can't see you now.'

John and the other children stood still. 'Please, sir, we've come a long way,' said John.

'Couldn't they just see him?' a mother said. 'Couldn't he just touch the children? Just put his arms round them? We wouldn't take up much of his time.'

'I'm sorry,' said the man, who had been joined by another. 'Jesus is too tired. You must come back another day.'

Hannah turned away so that the men wouldn't see that she was trying not to cry. John had run to Mother.

Then another voice called, 'Let the children come to me. I love to see them, at any time.' It was Jesus! He really wanted to see them! The children rushed forward again, right into his arms!

'Don't ever stop them coming,' Jesus said to his friends. 'These children belong to God just as much as the grown-ups. I'm always pleased when they want to see me.'

Hannah looked up at his face. She felt his kind hand on her shoulder. She knew he loved children.

Colour

Project outline

By the time they are five-and-a-half most children know the names of colours, but they have been aware of colour from a much earlier age. Exploring different aspects of colour, and only a few can be touched on here, will increase this awareness and can lead to a sense of wonder in God's variety of creation.

Favourite colours should be selected as a starting point for this project and a block graph made. Painted or covered matchboxes can be used for this, or simply squares of coloured paper. Display this later at the assembly. If the school encourages the children to group objects into 'sets', as a beginning to mathematics, this type of work will already be familiar. A tray, or enclosed group, of blue objects becomes a 'set'. Such sets can be positioned round the class-room, or drawn or chalked on paper. For older children these sets of coloured objects can be subdivided or sectioned as further mathematical exercises.

Colours suggested by the seasons can be talked about and illustrated, eg, the oranges and browns of autumn leaves, the blue sky of spring, the grey and white of winter, and the multitudinous colours of summer. Simple experiments with light, water and prisms could be done to reproduce the colours of the spectrum, and these could be related to the colours of the rainbow.

If time allows, camouflage in animals and insects could be discussed and researched. It would also be interesting to discuss colours used by soldiers for camouflage, in uniforms, buildings, planes and lorries, etc. This could be compared with the brightly-coloured uniforms of soldiers as little as a hundred years ago.

The three primary colours — red, blue and yellow — could be talked about, and experiments in mixing these colours — in paint, transparent paper, or light — done and recorded.

Interest in the colour of hair, eyes and skin will probably give rise to more graph work. Talk together, too, about certain colours evoking feelings of happiness, sadness, warmth, anger and so on. Art work comes naturally from thinking about such things, and will provide material for the assembly.

Awareness of colours in our surroundings is one thing; imagining a world without any colour is another. To stimulate imagination in this respect, the teacher should pass round a few pairs of dark glasses. Although colour through these will not be entirely absent, it will be sufficiently dimmed to make the children realise what a dull world it would be without colour. Looking through the glasses at the blue sky or a yellow flower would bring home to the children the brightness and clearness of God's world. Black and white television or photographs or book illustrations emphasise what we would miss if there was no colour. The children could draw with white chalk on black paper, or vice versa, and show these to the school.

If the children are old enough, they could write their own poems or stories about colour, or on subjects such as 'Inside a green forest', or 'The colours in my bedroom', or 'The purple dragon'. The best of these should be read in the assembly.

The assembly

Hymns and songs

All things bright and beautiful	NCS 4 and 5
O lovely world of colour	NCS 23
Think of a world without any flowers	SSL 15
I love God's tiny creatures	SSL 42

Poem
I like red, it's warm and bright,
It's like a bonfire on Guy Fawkes night.
I like blue, it's the colour of sky,
Or the sea, or a lake, or a stream going by.
I like green in the tree tops tall,
And the grass in the park where I play with my ball.
But best I like yellow, the colour of sun,
And daffodils dancing; it's the colour of fun.
My teddy bear's yellow, and little chicks too,
It makes me feel happy all the day through.

Music
Scherzo from *Colour Symphony,* Bliss
(Note: This movement from the symphony illustrates the colour red.)

Prayer

Thank you, God, for all the colours in your world. Help us to notice them and enjoy them, and to feel sorry for people who cannot see them.

Stories

Bible stories: Solomon's offerings — 1 Kings 7.48-51

Blind Bartimaeus — Mark 10.46-52

The legend of how the robin got his red breast, found in many books of Christian legends

The bad day and the rainbow (told in full)

The bad day and the rainbow

'What can we do?' Mark said, staring out of the window at the rain.

'I want to go out,' said Janet. 'Mother said we could go and play in Nana's garden today.'

'I've got wellington boots,' said Mark, 'and we could put our anoraks on.'

They went into the kitchen where Mother was making cakes. 'When can we go to Nana's?' they asked.

'Well, you certainly can't go at the moment,' Mother said firmly. 'Nana won't want muddy footmarks and dripping raincoats all over her house.'

'She said we could play in the garden,' said Mark. 'She's got a tree I want to try to climb. I could put my Red Indian suit on.'

'I want to play Red Indians, too,' said Janet.

'Wait a minute!' said Mother. 'You're not going anywhere in all this rain. I'll phone Nana and tell her you might come over later on. But it will probably be too muddy, even then, to play outdoors.'

Mark and Janet went back to the living-room. The rain was still beating on the windows. It looked grey and miserable outside. It wasn't much better indoors: it was so dark they almost needed a light on.

They could hear Mother on the phone, explaining that it was too wet for them to walk over to Nana's house. 'Maybe later on,' she said, 'but let me know if Grandpa's any worse.'

'Grandpa's not feeling very well,' she told the children, 'perhaps it's best not to go at all today.'

'Oh no!' said Mark and Janet together. They were very disappointed. Nana and Grandpa had a lovely garden, with a big rockery and lots of little paths, and fruit trees, and a lovely rubbish dump.

There wasn't anything to do at home — not a thing! Only the same old toys to play with, the same old games, in the same old rooms. They sat around, bored, and the rain didn't stop. Even the smell of Mother's cooking

15

reminded them that the morning had gone and that dinner was near, and the rain still rained and the day was still grey and colourless.

It was nearly three o'clock when Janet noticed a break in the clouds. 'There's some blue sky,' she called, and Mark ran to look. They watched as the blue patch got bigger. 'Why doesn't the rain stop?' they asked each other. Suddenly from a break in the clouds the sun came shining through. All the colours in the garden showed up again.

'Hurrah!' they shouted and jumped up and down.

'But it's still raining,' Mark pointed out. 'Mother will never let us go!'

Just then Mother called from the kitchen. 'Come here, you two, quickly,' she pulled a chair up by the window for them to stand on.

Mark and Janet looked out. There in the sky, bright and clear against the dark clouds at the back of the house, was a rainbow — the biggest and the best that they had ever seen.

'I can see red and yellow and green,' said Mark.

'And orange and blue and mauve,' said Jane, 'and it stretches to nowhere, right across the houses and the trees.'

'Why do we have rainbows?' asked Mark. 'Where do they come from?'

Mother explained that when the sun shone through the rain the light split up into colours. 'They say that it's a promise from God,' she added, 'a promise that he will always care for us.'

Just then the phone rang and Mother went to answer it. She came back smiling.

'Grandpa's feeling much better,' she said.

'And the rain has stopped,' said Mark.

'Nana says you can go over as soon as you like,' Mother said. 'She says your bright sunny faces are just what Grandpa needs to see.'

Mark and Janet didn't take long to get ready.

'I'm glad we saw the rainbow,' said Janet, as they skipped along the road. 'I'll always remember it's a promise from God.'

Harvest

Project outline

With the autumn comes harvest, the time of gathering, assessing, storing and distributing the fruits of the land. We are reminded of the days when farmers met in the churches after the last of the grain was harvested, to offer to God gifts of fruit and vegetables and wheat, and to thank him for them. Nowadays Harvest Thanksgiving has a much wider interpretation. As we offer our gifts we are thanking God for riches of the earth that were unknown to man a few generations ago; for riches of men's minds, too: for discoveries and inventions, for works of creation and interpretation, and for explorations into the heavens, the earth and under the sea.

There are many ways in which a project could be built around harvest, many aspects which could be explored and shared with the school. Some are given here for the teacher to think about; one of them may begin a line of thought leading to a very worthwhile project. A topic on 'Water' is given in some detail for those who would like to follow it.

Aspects on harvest

(a) Where food comes from, eg packets and tins from different countries, therefore information and stories about the people living there. Make a display for the assembly.

(b) Where the food we collect at the harvest festival goes to; how it will be distributed and received, how the old people or other recipients, live and what more we can do for them. Make a chart or a diagram for the assembly.

(c) Since we have enough to eat, we should think of those who are starving, perhaps with reference to the work of Christian Aid and Oxfam.

(d) Our own offerings, of our talents, our love and our service.

Water   This is perhaps the most important of God's gifts, because without it the earth would be dry, barren, and completely lifeless. Drawings and paintings should be done by the children showing what earth would look like and displayed at the assembly. Everything needs water to live: people, animals and plants.

People   If we had no water in our bodies we should weigh less than half our normal weight. The children could demonstrate this to the rest of the school by drawing round a boy or girl, and making the outline clear and

17

heavy. More than half the outline could then be coloured in with blue paint, to represent water. People also need water for other purposes: for washing — ourselves, our clothes, our dishes, our cars, our roads, etc; for cooking — look at recipes which need water added, or water being used to boil or steam dishes, or food itself in which water is present. People need water to enable some things to work: refrigerators, some central heating systems, lavatories, etc. Water is needed for power, in factories, mills and so on. Water also gives people a lot of pleasure, and the children will be able to think of things like swimming, fishing, rowing, sailing and snowballing. During all the discussions and discoveries that the children make, the teacher will find ways of turning the talk into activity and doing into display, ready for the assembly.

Plants and animals   Probably the use of water by people will be enough for the class to tackle, but should a fuller project be needed, the teacher could extend it to include plants and animals. She should lead the class to think about plants needing water, and do experiments with growing seeds in connection with this; also talk about plants that actually grow in water: reeds, bulrushes, and crops such as rice. Animals, too, could not live without water to drink, and some actually make their homes in water, eg pond creatures, whales, jellyfish (which are almost wholly composed of water), and fish. Others need water for swimming: birds such as ducks and swans; and animals such as sealions and otters.

At harvest time, whatever the subject of the project, it would be as well to conclude by thinking of those who, through lack of water, lack of funds or resources, or lack of knowledge, are always hungry. We, who have enough, should find out how to share, and it is never too early to begin to show children how this could be done.

The assembly

Hymns and songs

God sends the water — we call it rain	NCS 8
Ears of corn are waving	NCS 22
First the seed	NCS 24
When the corn is planted	SSL 55
The farmer comes to scatter the seed	SSL 56

Poem

It's raining.
Great drops of water
Are falling from the sky,
A grey sky,
A low-down sky.
The raindrops
Bounce,
Up and down on the ground,
Hard rain,
Racing down the roof,
Tearing past the leaves,
Pelleting on the path.

The grasses and flowers
Bow down,
Whipped into submission
By a watery master.
But that same master,
Soaking deep into the earth,
Feeds and lifts the flowers again;
Until, tall,
Beautiful and bright,
They wait
To be quenched again.

Music

Slow movement from *Symphony No 6 (Pastoral)*, Beethoven

Prayer

If there is a harvest display, use this as a focal point for the prayer, with the children looking at it as they pray.

Thank you, Father God, for the wonderful things you give us. We thank you for our food, our clothes, and our homes. We want to share with other people all that we have brought today. Help them to be happy too.

Stories

Bible stories: Ruth in the harvest field — Ruth 1.1-9, 16-19; 2.1-9,17
Parable of the sower — Matthew 13.3-9
The greatest gift (told in full)

The greatest gift

Polly looked at the rain. It cascaded down the shed roof and dripped on to the ground. It swept the window, and ran in wide ribbons down to the sill.

'Can I go out?' Polly asked her mother.

'Of course not!' Mother said.

Polly sighed. She supposed it had been a silly question, but did it really matter if she got wet? She could put her boots on, and her mackintosh with a hood. She got wet when she had a bath, didn't she? And Mother washed her hair once a week. And her clothes got wet when they were washed.

It had rained yesterday, too, when they went out shopping. Mother had been quite cross. She had put up her umbrella and walked very quickly to the

19

bus stop. Polly would have liked to walk slowly so that she could splash in the puddles, or stand with her mouth wide open, catching the rain.

Today, Polly was cross; the rain was making her stay indoors. She wanted to go out to play. Polly was cross all the afternoon. And when she was cross, Mother became cross again, and then Father became cross when he came home from work. Mother decided that Polly had better go to bed early.

Next day was Sunday, and Polly knew that she would go out, even if it rained, because their church was holding its harvest festival service. She had a basket of fruit ready to take, and she had polished the apples until they shone.

The morning began well, for the sun was shining. 'I don't think it will last,' said Father gloomily, looking at the sky. 'Take an umbrella with you.'

Before Mother and Polly had gone very far down the road, the sun went in, and the rain began again. Just a few drops at first, and then more heavily. Mother put up her umbrella. Polly began to feel cross again. This time she could see no fun at all in getting wet. She covered her harvest basket with her coat. 'I hate the wet!' she said.

'I hope it won't spoil the harvest festival,' said Mother.

Inside the church Polly sat with her basket on her lap.

'We are here to thank God,' said the vicar, 'for all his gifts at harvest time.'

After a hymn, Polly carried her basket to the front where other people were placing theirs. She looked at the table right in the centre of the display. A huge loaf of bread and a large sheaf of wheat stood in front of it, and all round were flowers, fruit and vegetables. Right in the middle of the table, all by itself, was a glass, and in the glass was water.

'Water!' thought Polly. 'We can do without that!' And she thought of all the rain during the last few days.

Later, the vicar stood by the table and held the glass of water in his hand. 'This is really the most important of God's gifts to us,' he said. 'Without it nothing would live: no people, or animals, or plants.'

He explained how important water was to all living things. He said that there were many countries where there was never enough water, where the grass was dry and brown, where animals died, and where men, women and children cried because they never had enough to eat.

After the service Polly and her mother stood at the church door. The rain was coming down as heavily as ever. Polly stepped out into it, and lifted up her face so that she could feel the cold wet drops as they fell. She opened her mouth and let the raindrops fall on her tongue.

It felt wonderful to be wet, after all.

Trees

Project outline

Trees, familiar to both town and country children, make an interesting topic which leads easily into an assembly.

The children should be encouraged to look at the trees in their immediate neighbourhood, and samples of leaves could be brought to school and discussed: are they smooth or rough, serrated or plain, single or multiple in design? Do the colours vary from species to species, or within the species? For the child who can read, identifying these leaves from reference books can be fun. Make charts by drawing round leaves and labelling them. The teacher should make full use of the range of art and craft work, by making montages, leaf prints, pressed leaves, bark rubbings, drawings and paintings.

Having spent a little time on leaves and the trees from which they come, the focus should be centred on the uses that trees have for man and beast. Standing beneath a tree the children will probably have noticed birds making use of the tree for shelter, food or nesting. Any abandoned bird's-nests brought into the class-room can be shown in the assembly. It should be pointed out that birds need trees for the protection of their young, and therefore they should be left in peace, especially when nesting. If there is time, and the subject is suitable to the environment, a similar study could be made of squirrels, mice, and other woodland creatures.

The children will be able to think of ways in which man uses trees, and some suggestions for enlarging upon this project are given here: the use of trees for decoration and beauty — landscaping, and Christmas trees; trees for recreation and enjoyment — climbing, swinging, old tree trunks, etc; trees used for their timber — building, furniture, toys, etc; trees used for paper making, and the different types of paper and their uses; and food and fuel from trees — fruit, nuts, cocoa, rubber, etc. The list of topics could go on and on. If one of these subjects is chosen to work on, keep all suitable work, written, pictorial, recorded or collected, and use it during the assembly.

Making something from wood (balsa wood is ideal for Infants) is not too hard. Simple musical instruments from wood blocks, or the use of matchboxes and matchsticks, could fit into the project well and be demonstrated at the assembly. For some children the building of a castle from their own building blocks would be sufficient.

The assembly

Hymns and songs

God made the world	NCS 3
God, who made the earth	NCS 6
God made the iron, shiny grey	NCS 13
Who's that sitting in the sycamore tree?	SSL 32

Poem

The big old tree

There's a tree in the park that's big and round,
There aren't many other trees around;
There are swings, and a pool for paddling feet,
There's an ice-cream man and a wooden seat.
I go to the park at half past three,
And I say hello to the big old tree.
My friends all go to the park for a run,
Or a lolly-ice when there's lots of sun.
And their mothers sit on the wooden seat
While the babies paddle for a special treat;
But the big old tree gets quite ignored,
And I hug it then so it won't get bored —
And I'm sure the leaves smile down at me,
When I go to the park to visit the tree.

Music
Fantasia on Greensleeves, Vaughan Williams

Prayer
Thank you, Lord, for the strong trees which give us shade and shelter and whose wood is useful to people everywhere. Help us to look after all living, growing things.

Stories

Bible stories: King Hiram of Tyre helps King Solomon — 1 Kings 5.1-11; 6.14-18

The tree that helped someone — Luke 19.1-10 (told in full)

The first Christmas tree (from books on Christian legends)

The tree that helped someone

Long ago, in the country where Jesus lived, there was a man named Zacchaeus. He was a little man; he was so small that he had to stand on tiptoe to look out of the windows of his big house, and when he went for a walk, everyone could see that he was only as big as the children who played in the streets. He was also a greedy man. His job was to collect money from the people to give to the Romans. But he collected far more than the Romans needed, and he kept all the rest for himself. So he became very rich and spent the money on his beautiful big house, and fine clothes, and lots of food. But the thing that Zacchaeus wanted more than anything was something he couldn't go out and buy in a shop — even if he had all the money in the world. He wanted a friend. Nobody ever spoke to Zacchaeus; nobody ever came and walked with him along the street, and nobody ever came to supper with him.

One day he heard a noise outside his house, and he stood on tiptoe by the window so that he could see what was going on. Lots of people were hurrying past, some running, some walking very quickly, and they were all talking together. 'If we go up the road we shall be able to see Jesus,' they were saying.

Now Zacchaeus had heard of Jesus. He had once heard someone say that Jesus was a friend to everybody. 'If only he would be my friend,' he thought, as he hurried outside. He bustled along the street on his little legs until he came to a place where there was a crowd of people. But the people in front of him were so tall. Zacchaeus stood on tiptoe, but he couldn't see a thing. He tried looking round the people, and between them, but it was no good; he just couldn't see. He looked all round for a stone to stand on, but they were so small that they wouldn't have made him much taller. And then he looked up at the tree near him. It had big strong branches and lovely thick leaves. If he could climb that tree he could hide up there, and then, when Jesus came along and walked underneath, Zacchaeus would see him easily. And he *did* want to see this man who was everybody's friend.

Zacchaeus looked round to see if anyone was watching, but the people were all busy. They were calling out to their friends that Jesus was very near, and they didn't even notice the little man climbing up the tree like a monkey! Zacchaeus swung himself on to a branch that jutted out over the road and lay

23

very still, almost hidden by the leaves. He could see Jesus coming, young, tall and friendly-looking. He seemed to have plenty of friends, because he was smiling and talking to so many people.

Suddenly he moved right under Zacchaeus' tree, and stopped. Zacchaeus kept very quiet and still up in the branches of the tree. What would happen if Jesus suddenly looked up and saw him? The people down below would be sure to tell him what a greedy little man Zacchaeus was, and then he certainly wouldn't have a friend! He waited, almost afraid to breathe. And then Jesus *did* look up straight into Zacchaeus' face! He smiled, but Zacchaeus didn't dare to smile back.

'Come on down, Zacchaeus!' Jesus called — he even knew his name! 'I want to come to your house. Will you give me a meal?'

Zacchaeus began to scramble down, slipping and sliding until he was beside Jesus. He could hear the people all round him muttering and grumbling. 'That greedy little man,' they were saying. 'Fancy Jesus wanting to go to his house!' Zacchaeus made himself as tall as he could and strode along beside Jesus.

'This way,' he said.

Then he suddenly realised how greedy he'd been to take all that money that didn't belong to him. Some of the people in that crowd had looked really poor — they couldn't spare the money. He shouldn't have done it at all. If he really wanted to be friends with Jesus he would have to pay the money back. And that's just what he did.

Prayer to use with this story

Dear Father God, thank you for the big strong tree that helped Zacchaeus to find a friend. Help us to be good friends, even to the boys and girls we don't like very much.

Autumn

Project outline

By mid-October autumn has transformed the landscape, and even town areas bear its marks. In parks and gardens the deciduous trees have changed colour and sudden gusts of wind send leaves flying. Autumn itself is too vast a subject for a short project, and the teacher will need to decide on which aspect of it to base her topic, especially if the topic is to be fitted into the week's normal activities so that it can culminate in a religious assembly. Given here are a few suggestions for themes that could be followed, complete within themselves, but also the core of much wider possibilities.

The colours of autumn   Look in detail at leaves and their colours, the golds and browns and yellows; and the colour of autumn skies — both variable, of course. The wise teacher will use the colours of leaves and weather as they are at the time of the project, NOT as she thinks they should be for the time of year. The colours of field grasses, and of autumn fruits and berries, can also be noted. Find colours in magazines or wallpaper sample books that match the natural colours of autumn, and use them to make collages or friezes; or mix paint as nearly as possible; this is something that could be done with older children. Press and display autumn leaves, and make collections of fruit and berries to show at the assembly. Small children will need to be warned about the dangers of eating berries or seeds. Leaf prints or rubbings could be made using autumn leaves.

Seeds and their distribution   What happens to the pips or seeds of eating apples and pears in the autumn? Who, besides humans, collect blackberries, bilberries, hips or elderberries? With the children look round gardens at lupin seeds, and at seeds on other flowering plants — sunflowers, sweet peas, poppies. Note those that are distributed by expulsion. Discover together the properties of the winged seeds of sycamore and lime, and of dandelion clocks and the white whiskers of 'Old man's beard'. Drawings of these types of distribution can be made, plasticine models of them shown, and collections of them made for display. The theme of the assembly could be God providing for the coming year, making sure that life carries on.

Preparing for winter   God's care for his creatures and for all living things in his world is the theme for this project. The children should note signs of approaching winter: the falling leaves, changing weather, dying flowers, migration of summer-visiting birds. We all prepare for winter: wild animals either hibernate or prepare stores of food, and autumn berries provide the birds with extra food at a time when insects are scarce; humans buy extra clothing — mother knits woollen jumpers and puts extra blankets on the beds; father orders fuel, and bulbs for the garden, etc. Dogs, cats and other animals grow extra hair or fur to combat the cold. Country schoolchildren could find out how farmers and market gardeners prepare for winter. What changes in routine do fishermen or other outdoor workers (such as zoo attendants) have to make to be ready for the colder or wetter weather? Scrapbooks, friezes, lists, and pieces of creative writing should be prepared and shown at the assembly.

Other subjects worthy of consideration for short topics are the weather of autumn; hibernation, spiders and insects; and bird migration.

The assembly

Hymns and songs

Autumn leaves are falling down	NCS 21
O lovely world of colour	NCS 23
Look for signs that summer's done	SSL 54
When the corn is planted	SSL 55

Poem   **The wind**

Last night the wind blew so strongly,
    I could hear it outside in the trees,
I was glad of the blanket upon me
    Covering my nose to my knees.

Leaves rustled and chattered loudly,
    Some brushed on my window pane;
They were going somewhere without me,
    And would never come back again.

'Follow the wild wind of autumn',
    They called as they tapped and were gone.
I'd love to have run out and caught them,
    But they'd left me indoors alone.

I dreamt I was flying behind them,
  I watched as they whirled, gold and red,
I followed but knew I'd not find them
  Before I woke up in my bed.

Perhaps when I next hear the wind blow,
  And the leaves are all golden and red,
I'll wait for their tap at my window,
  And get out of my lovely warm bed —

I'll fly with them, twirling and dancing,
  As they twist and tumble and fall;
I'll go with them jumping and prancing,
  At the very first wild wind's call.

Prayer

O God, your world looks beautiful; we look up and see the colours of the trees and sky.

O God, your world sounds wonderful; we listen to the wind and the crunch of dry leaves as we walk through them.

O God, your world feels interesting, as we hold smooth conkers and knobbly acorn cups.

O God, your world smells and tastes lovely: with smoky garden bonfires and the special tastes of new apples and freshly picked blackberries.

Thank you for your world of Autumn.

Stories

Bible story: Jesus in the cornfields — Matthew 12.1-8

How autumn leaves helped a squirrel (told in full)

How autumn leaves helped a squirrel

It was the first time Tippit, the squirrel, had seen the leaves falling off the trees. He sat on a branch of the tree at the bottom of the garden and watched. The wind blew hard at the top of the tree, and teased the leaves from the branches above him.

When Tippit had first explored the tree from his squirrel's home high in the branches, the leaves had been small. They were tender, and were the brightest green of any in the garden. As Tippit grew, so the leaves grew, larger, and darker, and stronger. Tippit was glad of them when the rain came down. He hardly got wet at all. And when the sun was very hot he was glad of the leaves because they kept him cool. In between the leaves he had

27

learnt to walk and climb and jump. He had left his warm nest in the summer and learnt how to look for food. And now the leaves were falling down. He watched them twirling round and round as the wind caught them, until they rested on the ground below.

Tippit scrabbled down the tree trunk. He wanted to play with the leaves. They were not green any longer; they were brown and gold and yellow. He jumped into them. Some of them were so dried up that they crackled under his weight. He flicked his bushy grey tail, and the leaves leapt up again and danced round once or twice. Then they fell back to the ground, too tired to dance any more. Tippit was sad. Some of the leaves had curled up, some lay flat and wet in the puddles on the path under the tree. Tippit pushed his nose into a little pile of brown leaves near the trunk of the tree.

'Play with me! Play with me!' he cried. But the leaves only rustled together and made a bigger pile. Tippit tossed some into the air and the wind lifted them further along the path.

'Don't go!' Tippit called. 'We're friends, aren't we?'

He burrowed into another mound of leaves. 'Keep me warm,' he whispered, and the leaves seemed to close round him, sheltering his back from the cold wind. And as Tippit nosed further into the pile of leaves he found a cosy warm hole. It was just at the bottom of the tree, where the trunk went into the ground. Tippit looked round inside the hole. It was dark and secret, right under the pile of leaves. Just the place to store his nuts for the winter! He would put a pile of hazel cobs in this corner, and a heap of beech nuts over there. He scurried out under cover of the autumn leaves. 'Thank you, thank you,' he chattered to them as he passed through them. 'I'd never have found that little store-place without your help!'

His larder was soon filled with food. Tippit knew that many times in the winter he would wake up from one of his short naps and need to eat. What a good thing the leaves had shown him where to store the nuts!

Our bodies

Project outline

Small boys and girls often vie with each other in competitions of strength and prowess. At the Infant stage they are still stretching themselves — discovering new achievements and finding limits to their physical abilities. This project, from which an assembly leads easily and with meaning, can do much to give a sense of confidence and satisfaction to a slightly nervous child. It can also bring the over-confident extrovert child down to a level that other children can cope with. It will be useful, from the start, to let each child keep a personal record book alongside the class graphs and pictorial records of their different sizes and abilities which will be displayed at the assembly.

New discoveries for the children will be those of height, weight, and size of hands and feet, both their own and those of their class-mates. Simple exercises in measurement, classification and comparison will give valuable mathematical experience. If the weather is fine the children should take the opportunity to be in the field or playground when no one else is there. They will enjoy seeing how far each can throw a ball, how high each can jump, and how far each can stride. These exercises will all give more practice in measurement; pacers, metre rules or other class-room equipment may be used.

Similarities and differences in colour of eyes, skin and hair should be recorded. Self-portraits, made with the help of mirrors or baking foil, reveal much to the perceptive teacher. At certain times in a child's development different physical features will become important for him or will have been newly discovered. These will be emphasised by him by showing them either in great detail or size. The method of portrayal and the actual finished product will tell the teacher much about the child's attitude towards himself. For instance, his manner of attacking the picture, the features he chooses to paint first, and the colours he uses, all demonstrate this attitude.

If there is time the project can be extended in many directions. Probably the most valuable, as far as a religious assembly is concerned, would be further work on how to look after our bodies. This could include work on teeth — preventive measures of cleaning and sensible eating and regular visits to the dentist; on hair — the necessity for brushing, washing, etc; and on general health — balanced eating, exercise, sleep, cleanliness etc. Charts recording the children's discoveries should be made.

When the time for the assembly comes there should be ample material for showing to the school and for talking about.

The assembly

Hymns and songs

For all the strength we have	NCS 30 SSL 16
Let's all dance round while we're singing	NCS 97
Clap, clap, clap, clap	NCS 100
O Jesus, we are well and strong	SSL 40

Poem

On the slide

I climb up the steps of the slide,	I stand, I stretch, I laugh,
I sit at the top	Then turn and run again.
And look at the world,	I hop on the lowest metal step,
Then I flop,	Then it's up to the sun again.
Legs straight, down the other side.	Up, sit, slide, stop,
Quickly I go, and quicker,	Then climb again to the very top.
The ground is suddenly near,	I'm sure skiing, or diving,
Then slowly	Or flying,
I straighten	Is like what I do
And come to a	When I climb up the steps,
Stop;	Look round at the world,
'I'm down again, Mum, I'm here!'	Then slide down again
	To you.

Prayer

Every day, Lord Jesus, we are growing bigger. Every day we can do more things, we can walk further, run faster, and jump higher. Every day we are growing stronger. Help us to grow kinder and more loving too.

Stories

Bible stories: The man with the withered arm — Luke 6.6-10

The lady with the bent back (Old Sarah) — Luke 13.10-13

(told in full)

Old Sarah

Everyone in the village knew old Sarah. She lived in a little white house with a flat roof. There were stairs on the outside of the house, leading up to the roof. Nearly all the houses in the village were like that, and every evening mothers, fathers and children, and often grannies and grandpas too, climbed the stairs and sat on the roof. Then they talked together and watched the sun setting over the hills. During the day the women took their trays of bread dough up there to rise, or spread out grapes to dry in the sun.

It was a long time since old Sarah had used the stairs outside her little white house. They were quite overgrown with weeds that grew between the stones. Her flat roof was never used, and it was only brushed clean when her neighbour, who was already very busy, could spare the time to do it.

The older people in the village could remember when old Sarah used to climb her stairs every day like the other women. They could remember when she used to call cheerily from her roof to her friends across the narrow street. But old Sarah hadn't gone upstairs for years now. At first she had had pains in her legs and then pains in her back and in her arms, and over the years she had become bent and slow. Now she could only walk by leaning on two sticks.

'Here comes old Sarah,' the children would say, clearing a space for her to pass. Her head was bent so low she couldn't see far in front of her, and bumped into things unless she was helped. Everyone felt sorry for her, and mothers took her arm when she went to the well. Always one of the stronger girls carried her water jar back to the house.

Sometimes the sky over the village was patterned with white clouds, some-times it was the clearest blue; in the evening the sunset made it pink and gold; and at night it was bright with stars. Old Sarah never saw it, but she didn't grumble much. She had been bent for so long she had become used to it, and she didn't think she would ever be any better. Instead, her bones became stiffer and more crooked the older she got.

Every week a girl called Rachel, and her brother Amos, called at old Sarah's house to help her climb the hill to the synagogue, where the people went to worship God. Old Sarah wanted to praise God in spite of her poor bent bones.

'It is good to give thanks to the Lord,' she sang with the other people in the synagogue, 'for his love lasts for ever.'

One week Rachel and Amos helped old Sarah up the hill as usual, guiding her past the well and up the rough pathway to the synagogue.

'The lilies are in blossom,' said Sarah, her eyes looking at the path. 'That means the corn will be ripe soon.' Old Sarah saw a lot, even though she could only see the ground. She showed Rachel and Amos little insects scurrying from one blade of grass to another, and she never missed the tiniest blue flowers hidden in the clumps of thistles. But today Rachel and Amos wouldn't let her stop to look at the spiders' webs, or to point out the shiny white pebbles by the edge of the path.

'Jesus is coming to the synagogue,' Amos explained. 'There won't be room to get in if we don't hurry!'

Inside the synagogue it was cool and dark. Rachel led old Sarah behind the screen that separated the women and children from the men and boys. The building was already packed with people and Jesus was watching as Rachel and old Sarah tried to find a place to stand. He was talking to the other teachers, and looking at their law books. He found time to smile at Rachel.

'He smiled, old Sarah,' said Rachel. 'You couldn't see, but Jesus smiled at us.' Old Sarah strained to lift her head to see him, but it hurt her neck too much, and she stared at the floor again.

Suddenly everyone was quiet, waiting for Jesus, the visiting teacher, to begin speaking. As he read and spoke, Rachel listened and understood. Later he turned to the women's screen.

'Bring the old lady to me,' he called across to Rachel.

'He means you,' Rachel whispered to old Sarah, and they fumbled together to get past the people.

Old Sarah looked at the floor, and saw only Jesus' feet. 'You will get better,' his voice said. Sarah felt his strong hands upon her shoulders, and the strength from them seemed to leave his body and enter hers. Her bones straightened and she stretched her neck and her back and her arms and her legs. At last she lifted her head and looked into the face of Jesus — kind and full of love.

'I will lift up my eyes,' said old Sarah. 'Help comes from the Lord. Praise him!'

Rachel knew that Sarah was using words that were often sung in the synagogue, great words of praise.

'Praise the Lord!' said Rachel, as she left the synagogue with old Sarah, and 'Praise the Lord!' said old Sarah, as she walked down the hill, and for the first time in many years looked up at the wide blue sky.

People who help us

Project outline

This is a favourite theme for Infants, and one which every teacher will have tried at some time, perhaps under the title of 'Our Street', 'Our Town', 'The Services', 'Transport', etc. In such projects the children will have been introduced to people without whom their lives would be difficult or perhaps impossible, and who contribute greatly towards their well-being and comfort.

Talk about home and the family — the starting point of many successful topics — and let the children examine ways in which help is given and by whom. This will vary from household to household. Be aware of any children in the class who live in deprived conditions, or in a children's home. Some may even live in communities: many immigrant families live with several generations and branches of the family under one roof. The topic will need to be adapted to meet the special needs of such children. Certainly approach the subject of help for each other within the home with no pre-conceived notions or ideals — not every household practises what can be termed as unselfish service by all. In many, the service will be seen by the boys and girls to be given by the mother alone. Father's contribution of help by means of working to provide money so that the family might live, and enjoy living, should be pointed out. Drawings and writings about family help can be used to show the school at the assembly, and the children will enjoy acting the various roles.

The project should be enlarged to bring in the immediate tradespeople who help, eg, the milkman, postman, newspaper delivery girl or boy, dustman, etc. Try to explore in some depth what we should have to do without, and what we should have to do for ourselves, if these people did not serve us.

Perhaps the class, or groups from within the class, could visit a local shop to experience the service given to the community by shop assistants. It would be a good opportunity to point out to the children the responsibility they, as customers, should have towards the shop and the assistants there.

Teachers should make as much use as possible of the local situation: where there is a factory, a worker from it could be invited to visit the class to talk about what is made there; where there is a hospital, a whole project on health-help might be embarked upon as a subsequent exercise. If farming is predominant in the area, a different kind of help will emerge: that given by those who grow or produce food for us. Similar divergencies can develop in seaside communities, newly-developed areas or university towns. Whatever the approach, the teacher should keep bringing the children's thoughts back to the help that is given and received, and the interdependence of one group upon another. Merely making a note of the service given is not enough for an assembly service — the teacher should seek to plant in each child a seed of recognition of that help, and an overwhelming and spontaneous gratitude towards the giver.

There is no need to enlarge further upon the activities, written records and drawings that could accompany such a topic and be used at the assembly; these will come naturally as the subject is explored. They will also depend upon the amount of time being spent on it.

The assembly

Hymns and songs

'Click' goes the switch	NCS 33
I'd like to be a milkman	NCS 34
What do we see when we go to the town?	NCS 35
We thank you, heavenly Father	NCS 41

Poem

Helpers

Mothers are always there to help,
And Fathers are big and strong,
And Nannies and Grandads listen and love,
Specially when things go wrong.

Up in the town the people work,
And out on the deep blue sea,
And busy on farms all over the land
People are helping me.

Some work in the sky, some travel,
And some are deep underground;
You'd never believe when I counted,
The number of helpers I found.

Each of them serves me every day
And I want them all to know
I'd like to say 'Thank you', if only I could,
For working to help me so.

Prayer

We want to say thank you, God, for all the people who help us.

For our mothers and fathers, and our homes; for the food they prepare, for the clothes they buy, and for all the work they do to make us comfortable:

Thank you, God.

For people who help us every day when we are in school, learning or playing or having our dinner; for those who keep the school clean for us, and make it a safe place to be in:

Thank you, God.

For the men and women who serve us in the streets and in the shops; for those who drive our buses and mend our roads; for those who care for us when we are ill, and for those who give us television programmes:

Thank you, God.

Help us, dear God, to look for ways of serving other people.

Stories

Bible stories: Help given by a little girl — 2 Kings 5.1-14
　　　　　　　Jesus the helper: Jairus' daughter — Mark 5.21-24, 35-43
Thank you! (told in full)

Thank you!

Peter was watching the dustmen — big men who shouted to each other as they strode up the garden paths near his house. Then, with the bins swung onto their shoulders, they returned to the cart and emptied the rubbish into the rumbling, rolling mass of paper, tins and bottles. What a lovely job, Peter thought. To get paid for getting dirty and wearing old clothes and throwing things away!

He always stood by the gate on Thursday mornings in the holidays, waiting for the huge dustcart to come round the corner. It stopped in the middle of the road near his house. A big man with ginger hair always collected and emptied his particular dustbin. But this Thursday morning, when the men tumbled down from the cart and spread out into the houses along the road, laughing and shouting, the big ginger man wasn't there.

'Don't forget to do Jock's bins!' shouted one of the men to another.

'I'll do ours for you!' said Peter, rushing to the dustbin at the side of his house. It was very heavy — however had Mother found all that rubbish in one week? It was no good thinking he could sling it on to his shoulders; he wondered if he would ever be strong enough for that. He pulled it by the handles and dragged it a little way. The lid fell off with a loud clatter. Some flies flew up into his face — nasty black, buzzing flies. He didn't like them at all, and he remembered how he'd seen lots of wasps last summer, hovering round the dustcart as the men emptied the bins. He wondered if they often got stung.

The dustbin shifted about a metre as he pulled. He put his head down to pull again. What a horrid smell! He couldn't believe it! How could anyone choose to work with that smell every day? At that moment the bin tipped a little too far as he pulled on the handles, and the screwed up paper and cereal boxes on the top fell on to the path. Now Peter could see the rotten apple cores, the wet potato peelings, and the custard his baby brother had refused to eat yesterday. And there were the chicken bones and the greens he had left on his plate two days ago. And the chipped plate Mother had thrown away was there too. It might have given him — or the dustmen — a nasty cut.

He left the dustbin and went into the kitchen. 'I hate dustbins!' he said to his mother, who was cutting up fruit for his lunch. 'Those dustmen must be stupid, doing a job like that!'

'Someone's got to empty the bins,' said his mother. 'Whatever should we do if no one took the rubbish away?'

Peter thought of how the old tins would pile up, and how the passage beside the house would begin to smell and attract hundreds of flies and wasps. It was a good thing that there were men who were willing to get filthy and work with all those nasty smells and put up with all those insects, Peter thought.

The very next Thursday he was out by the gate as usual. Ginger Jock was back and grinned at him as he went off down the path to fetch Peter's dustbin. 'Thank you very much!' shouted Peter as he watched Ginger Jock empty it into the back of the cart. And he really meant it.

Being thoughtful

Project outline

Few children are thoughtful of others unless they are often reminded. It is not unusual or unnatural for them to be concerned about themselves most of the time. They are discovering the world in so far as it relates to them; they have little concept of a horizon beyond that which they can see. Through the media, however, they are probably quicker to grasp some idea of the enormity of distance, and of life across the oceans, than were the children of a generation ago. But the self-interest of little children has hardly changed over the years.

The teacher may imagine that a long project on being thoughtful is hardly practicable; certainly there may not be much to show for it as far as activity work and display material is concerned. But launching into a project as abstract as this may be far more valuable than working on one whose message is more easily demonstrated.

Talking to the children, reminding them throughout this preparation period, of the needs of others, and pointing out situations in which thought is essential, will be enough. Use any instances of momentary kindness, or even thoughtlessness, observed in the class-room or playground as a starting point. Re-enact these instances with the children, and discuss them. Get the children to wonder where, when and how they could be thoughtful; perhaps Mother is tired when they get home, therefore extra thought could lead to the boy or girl being very quiet.

The first point to make, then, is that they should get used to looking at a situation, seeing what is required, using some thought, and acting upon it. The children might form small groups in the class-room and present short scenes of such situations to the rest of the class. From this point, go on to talk about the times when thought may be necessary to prevent something happening, eg, if children play with a ball too near a greenhouse, a pane of glass may easily get broken. Thought, at the right time, would make the participants move away to a safer area. Sometimes it is worth noting that thought may be required when other people are not directly involved: in not dropping litter at beauty spots, for instance. Show the children that this is also thought for others, and is important. Perhaps one of the most valuable things that the teacher can do at this time is to encourage the children's imagination, to be able to think how other people are feeling, and to act upon it. That is thoughtfulness of the best kind.

The boys and girls could act out one or two examples of thoughtfulness for the school. Some of the more articulate should explain them, or talk about circumstances when they themselves have needed to be thoughtful.

The assembly

Hymns and songs

Tell me the stories of Jesus	NCS 65
Hands to work and feet to run	SSL 21
When I needed a neighbour	SSL 35
Think, think on these things	SSL 38

Poem

Mummy looked tired

Mummy looked tired when she met me from school,
    I thought she seemed quiet and sad;
I wanted to help; I wanted to say,
    'Please, how can I make you glad?'
I thought I might carry her shopping home,
    But found it too heavy for me;
I wanted to tell her I loved her so,
    And how good I wanted to be.
I tried to be kind when we got back home;
    She was tired when we'd had our tea,
So I kissed her eyes and she fell asleep,
    While I sat there upon her knee.

Prayer

O God, let us be quiet and think about you; we know you love us and want us to follow you. We can do this by loving and helping other people. Show us what we can do for them.

Stories

Bible stories: The expensive perfume — Mark 14.3-9
              Martha and Mary — Luke 10.38-42
The thoughtless Brownies (told in full)

The thoughtless Brownies

Sharon was old enough to be a Brownie-Guide. Her sister Anne had been one for a year already, and Sharon knew all about the things that Brownies did. She had practised their special salute, she knew the law and promise, and Mummy had bought her a uniform. She had been going to Brownies for two months now, and loved it. Anne had four badges sewn on her sleeve, and Sharon wanted to earn some as well. Brown Owl, who was the leader of the Brownies, had been teaching the younger girls all they needed to know for a badge called the 'Hostess' badge; they had to be able to lay a table and make a cup of tea, and one or two other things that would show they could invite someone in for tea.

'We're all ready to do the test for our "Hostess" badge, Brown Owl,' said Sharon and her friends Paddy and Christine.

'Very well,' said Brown Owl. 'Mrs Kay comes to test you for that badge. I'll ask her if she's free next Friday.'

When she got home, Brown Owl phoned Mrs Kay. 'Can you come along to Brownies next Friday?' she asked her. 'I've got three of my younger girls who want to take their "Hostess" badge, and I'd like you to come along and test them. I'll have everything ready.'

Mrs Kay said she would come. On Friday, after work, Brown Owl put on her uniform, ready to go to Brownies.

'I shall have to get there early tonight,' she told her husband, as she left him to do the washing-up. 'I've got three of my Brownies taking their "Hostess" badge test. I must take this china and cutlery with me. Oh, and a tablecloth. I wonder if there is enough milk down at the hall?'

She was very busy collecting everything together. When she arrived at the hall where the Brownie meetings were held she was busy again, moving tables and chairs so that Mrs Kay would have a little corner in which she could test the three Brownies.

Meanwhile, Sharon had put on her uniform, and washed her hands and face. She was just going out of the front door when she saw Paddy and Christine going past. But they weren't in uniform.

'You'll be late!' Sharon called.

Paddy and Christine turned round. Sharon noticed that they hadn't even been going in the direction of the hall, which was only a little way from her house.

'Oh, we've decided not to go this week,' Paddy said. 'There's a very good programme on television. It won't matter if we miss just one week.'

'Oh well,' said Sharon, 'I'm not going without you.' And she went back indoors and changed into her jeans.

39

Mrs Kay had already arrived at the hall with her notebook and pencil. She had thought of a lot of questions to ask the girls. Brown Owl had shown her the box of cutlery and china, and told her where the tea, milk, and sugar were kept. She was quite tired by the time the Brownies arrived at six o'clock. Mrs Kay waited for Sharon and Paddy and Christine. She waited and waited.

She and Brown Owl had gone to a lot of trouble and spent a lot of time getting ready for those three Brownies. What a pity they had been so thoughtless!

Caring for the sick

Project outline

The Public Health Service is not a subject one would think touches an Infant child closely. Yet all through their lives small children have been personally in contact with healers and those trying to prevent disease. The teacher should establish, early on in the project, where the emphasis is to lie. It could be on sick people and places of healing, ie people who need medical and surgical help, and the hospitals, clinics, old people's and convalescent homes to which they can go. Or it could be on the caring help given by those who tend the sick, not only the doctors and nurses, ambulance drivers and dentists, but the whole community — friends, neighbours and relatives — who are concerned for the welfare of the one in need. In either case, the teacher will want to feel that the children develop a more caring attitude towards sick people, and that caring is not only an attitude of mind but also an activity.

Start where the child meets sickness, or the healing agency, or the person who cares. Perhaps one of the children, or a near relative, has been ill or gone into hospital; or the visit of the school nurse or dentist could trigger off the project. Suggestions for topics linked to the general theme are given here for the teacher to select and expand or eliminate as she works out the topic to suit her particular class of children. Visits from people concerned, simple films, pictures, question and answer research for the older children, with plenty of creative activity, should be included in each smaller project if possible.

Clinics Many children accompany their mothers and younger brothers and sisters to the clinic. They see the health visitors and their helpers weighing, checking, and giving advice. They see children being immunised, injections being given, welfare foods being distributed. Home visits by health visitors and district nurses could be included in this section.

Hospitals Even if the child has no personal contact with a hospital, he or she will probably know where it is and what it is there for. The work of the nurses and orderlies can be looked at. (Don't forget to include the male nurse; many children still grow up with the idea that only girls enter the nursing profession.)

School Health work For a simple project, the health of the children in an Infant school could be sufficient on its own. Why does the dentist examine everyone's teeth? What can the nurse tell about eyes when she tests them? What are the injections given to some children for? Who cares for the children who injure themselves in the playground? What happens to those who feel ill at school? Learning about these things by asking the people concerned relevant questions and by observations, or by hearing someone come in to talk about them, will provide the basic topic work necessary for leading up to an assembly.

Each one of these topics could be a project on its own. Together and, if time permits with others added, they could make a meaningful and rewarding longer project. Pictures and written work should be displayed at the assembly, and some of the older children might talk about the people whose work they have investigated.

The assembly

Hymns and songs

When we are happy, full of fun	NCS 29
For all the strength we have	NCS 30
Look out for loneliness	SSL 36
O Jesus, we are well and strong	SSL 40

Poem

This could be said by two groups of children, or by teacher and children in turn.

Poor Andrew

Mummy, I don't feel very well.
My throat hurts,
And I feel funny all over.
Poor Andrew,
He's not very well.

Mummy, I want to go to bed,
I'm all cold,
And my back just won't stop shaking.
Poor Andrew,
He feels so ill now.

Mummy, I'm better lying down;
The bed's warm
And the pillow feels all cosy.
Poor Andrew,
The doctor's coming.

Mummy, the doctor had a torch;
I liked him;
And he looked in my ears as well.
    Poor Andrew,
    He'll soon be well.

Mummy, I'm better this morning,
I feel fine!
And I don't want to stay in bed.
    Andrew's great!
    He's well again.

Mummy, thank you for being here,
Loving me,
Helping to make me well again.

Prayer

Dear Father God, many people are ill; may they soon be well again.
Many people are old; please be with them and help them to be happy.
Many people are lonely; help me to smile at them.

Stories

Bible stories: The centurion's servant-boy — Matthew 8.5-13
                How Jesus wants us to live — Matthew 25.34-40
How Jason helped (told in full)

How Jason helped

Jason's mother had to go into hospital. The doctor had told her so a long time
ago. She had bought two lovely pink nightdresses, and Father had given her
a purple house-coat to wear when she was well enough to get out of bed. Jill,
Jason's sister, had bought her some talcum powder, and Jason had spent his
pocket money on a bar of sweet-smelling soap for her. Jason's other sister,
Liz, who was eleven, had painted Mother a little picture to put on her bedside
table.

'All these presents will help me to feel better very quickly,' Mother assured
them. 'And Daddy and Auntie Ruth will look after you well.'

Auntie Ruth said she would drive over from the town where she lived the
very same day that Mother went into hospital.

But when the day came, the plans began to go wrong. First, Daddy's car
wouldn't start, and he had to call a taxi to take Mother and him to the
hospital. And by the time Jill, Liz and Jason had said goodbye to Mother and
watched the taxi drive away they were all late for school. Jason didn't really
want to go to school at all, but Jill said he must. 'Auntie Ruth will be here
when you come home from school,' she said.

But when Jason arrived home from school old Mrs Wells, from next door,
was waiting for him. 'Your Auntie Ruth phoned me to say she's been delayed.
She's got such a bad cold that she doesn't feel well enough to drive all the way

from Dorchester. So I'll stay with you until Jill comes home from school, then you'll be all right until your father comes home.'

Jason was almost ready to cry. It was bad enough Mother being ill, and having to leave them to go into hospital, but now Auntie Ruth hadn't come. The house looked dark, and it was cold. Mrs Wells put the light on in the kitchen and boiled the kettle. 'I'll make you a nice cup of tea,' she said.

Jason didn't like tea, but he knew Mrs Wells was trying to be kind. He put the television on. Half an hour later he heard Jill and Liz come in.

Jill came into the room where Jason sat. 'I'm going to get supper ready,' she told him. 'You can help by laying the table.'

'What are we having?' asked Jason, hoping it would be sausages.

'Eggs, I think,' said Jill. Jason pouted. He wanted sausages; or perhaps fish and chips; or even baked beans. But not eggs. Mummy knew he didn't like eggs very much. He put the knives and forks on the table.

'Jason!' Liz called. 'Your room's in a mess! Come and clear it up!'

'I'm busy,' shouted Jason, fetching the salt and pepper quickly. He didn't want to clear up his room. Mummy usually helped him to do that.

Later, when Daddy came home, he told them that Auntie Ruth would have to spend another day at home, but she would come to look after them the day after next, if she was feeling better. Jason began to cry quietly into his cup of milk, but nobody seemed to notice. It was so awful... he hated Mummy being away... he didn't like Jill's cooking, and Liz certainly shouldn't tell him what to do all the time. He wanted to feel Mummy's warm arms; he wanted her cuddle, her kiss. He wouldn't even mind if she was cross with him just at that moment. If only she would come back. He wondered if she was really ill, she didn't seem to be. He wanted her back.

Jason got up and walked upstairs. It was awfully dark. Mummy usually put on the lights for him. She usually washed his knees and inspected his hands, and always, always, read him a goodnight story. Nobody would think of that tonight. He struggled into his pyjamas and lay down on his bed. The tears poured down his cheeks. 'Poor me,' he kept thinking. 'Poor me!'

Daddy opened the bedroom door and saw his tears. 'Oh Jason,' he said, ·'Mummy's going to be all right. Don't worry about her.'

Jason stopped crying. He'd forgotten what Mummy must be feeling like, all alone in a hospital bed. He had only been worrying about himself.

'You can help her to get better,' Daddy reminded Jason. 'You don't have to be a doctor or a nurse, you know. If Mummy thinks we are managing happily at home she will get better more quickly.'

Jason thought about it. Tomorrow would be different. He'd be happy and cheerful and helpful, and he'd be helping to make Mummy well again.

Christmas

Project outline

With all the Christmas activities going on in the school at this time, it is natural that an assembly should reflect the excitement and anticipation that everybody feels. Several suggestions are given for ways in which the Christmas stories could be presented. It is assumed that much work connected with the festive season is already in progress in the class-room. This being so, it is unnecessary to give ideas for any extra activities on the part of the class involved in the assembly. Four stories are given in note form, together with the biblical references for the Nativity story. Whichever story is chosen, the teacher should familiarise the class with it early on in the preparations. Discussions should begin on the best way to present it to the school. Here are some suggestions:

1 Pictures of the main points of the story (work these out with the class after the story has been told), painted by the children, should be held up as the story unfolds. The story might be told by the children, read from their own written versions of it, or from sentences provided by the teacher.

2 The story could be dramatised   The production should be managed by the children if they are old enough. The teacher will need to direct the thinking: 'What sort of a person was ...?' 'How can we make ... appear really old?' 'What can we use for costumes, props, scenery?' 'Do we really need these?' If small platforms or a dais are available, use them to make the playlet more interesting and visible to the rest of the school.

3 The play could be mimed as the teacher, or a child or children, read or tell it. Work out the exact movements so that the mime will clarify the story rather than confuse it.

4 The story could simply be told by the teacher   The class could introduce and teach a new carol to the school. Or they could have Christmas cards already prepared to give out to members of the staff, or children known to be ill, or old people living in a nearby home, or a hospital. If the Nativity story is told, the children might use coloured and cut-out paper models of a crib and assemble these as the story progresses.

In stories 2 and 3, 'candles' will be needed for acting or miming. Artificial ones can be made by drawing them on thick paper, and sticking fluorescent paper to the top as a flame; or by using cardboard tubes with brightly coloured tissue paper stuffed in the top.

Whatever is decided upon for the presentation of the Christmas assembly, plan it well and make sure the children are enthusiastic. Their excitement and anticipation will be conveyed to, and absorbed by, the rest of the school.

The assembly

Hymns and songs

Away in a manger, no crib for a bed	NCS 48
Softly sleeping, softly sleeping	NCS 49
Sing for the baby at Bethlehem	NCS 54
On Christmas Day, what do we see?	NCS 56

Any other Christmas carols known to the children

Poems

Two poems are given here, each composed by eight-year-old children. The children in the class might make up their own poems for the assembly, either writing them down, or speaking them into a tape recorder.

No more people
Today.
There's a stable
Some way away.
Go there with this lamp —
That way.

He who sleeps
In the manger
Is Jesus Christ.
Christ was born
This lonely night.
Come and see for he is King.

Mary holds her little baby
    Sweetly by his bed.
She kisses him on his small soft cheek,
    And strokes his tiny head.

Then from the East
    Came three wise men
Bringing precious gifts;
    They gave them to the King.

The shepherds came to worship him,
    To play their lowly part,
And Mary treasured all these things
    In her gentle heart.

Music
Christmas Concerto, Corelli
A ceremony of carols, Britten
Pastoral Symphony from *Messiah,* Handel

Prayer
Thank you, Jesus, for coming to live on our earth. Thank you for all the happy times we have at Christmas. Help us to remember you all through the coming year.

Stories
Bible story: The Nativity — Luke 2.1-20; Matthew 2.1-12
The story of St Nicholas
Christmas in Sweden
Christmas in Sarawak
The legend of the Christmas roses
(These four stories are given in note form for the teacher to enlarge. It must be remembered that, in common with all legends, there are many different versions of the St Nicholas story and that of the Christmas roses.)

The story of St Nicholas
Nicholas lived over 1600 years ago in Myra, Asia Minor, now known as Turkey. He was young, rich and kind. He gave money to those who needed it, but always in secret. A poor man in the same town had three daughters who had no money for the dowry to marry the men they loved. Nicholas knew they were unhappy and wanted to help. Wrapped in a dark cloak, he visited their house at night and left a bag of gold. Subsequently he left two more bags of gold, and the daughters, overjoyed, were able to marry. Nicholas often gave to the children, too, leaving toys and food on their doorsteps. It is said that when he grew old he had a long white beard. After his death he was made a saint. The Dutch people knew him as Sinterklaas, which became Santa Claus in our language.

Christmas in Sweden
Ingrid lives in a village in Sweden. She is excited about Christmas. She and her young brother open the door on the Advent calendar from December 1 onwards. On December 6 they leave their polished shoes outside their bedroom door for St Nicholas to fill with sweets. Father hangs a lighted star in the window of their house. They have a decorated Christmas tree in the middle of the room. The whole family dances round it; this is called the 'ring

dance'. Someone dresses as the *jultomte,* or Christmas gnome, a visitor from fairyland, and distributes the family presents. Later Ingrid dresses in her Lucia costume: a long white dress with a crown of evergreens and candles. She has to move slowly and carefully as the candles must be lit while she gives out cakes to the family. On December 13 she parades with other fair-haired girls of the village in their costumes for the Lucia Festival. Ingrid's brother goes out carol singing with a large group of boys called 'Star boys'. They dress in white, wearing hats decorated with stars. They act short nativity scenes, and one boy dresses up as a goat, to represent the devil.

Christmas in Sarawak

Sarawak is a territory in north-west Borneo. Much of the land is soft and wet, so the houses there are built on high poles to keep them out of the water. Jad lives in a 'longhouse' with several other families. They eat their meals together on the long verandah. At Christmas a pastor comes to each longhouse, and Jad is ready with his candle. After the service he and all the other children light their candles and carry them carefully down the ladders to the canoe-like boats. They go round the houses in them, singing carols. It is very warm. Jad loves hearing the singing coming from all the boats, and seeing the candles reflected in the water. At some houses they get out and climb up the ladders to watch firecrackers, which are like fireworks. All these things — the candles, the singing, and the crackle and brightness of the fire-works — make the welcome to the birthday of Jesus gay and colourful.

The legend of the Christmas roses

Pippa slept with her father and other shepherds on the hills outside Bethlehem. She woke to see a light in the sky and to hear singing. Father and the others were moving off towards the town. Pippa hurried to catch them up, but they were too quick. She peeped in at the stable where they were, and saw a baby in a manger, with his parents. Shepherds were kneeling and offering gifts. Pippa had no gift. She sat on the ground outside, and her tears fell to the ground. As they fell, small shoots, and then leaves, and then flowers, appeared. Pippa gathered a bunch and took them as her gift to the Christ-child. Legend says they were the first Christmas roses, like pale pink or white anemones.

The New Year

Project outline

In spite of the recent celebrations, this can be a depressing time of year. The Christmas holidays have seemed all too short to the teachers, and the anti-climax of after-Christmas weighs heavily upon the children. But there are forces working secretly at this time; it is a time of secret birth and re-birth. Children love secrets and will be fascinated by the thought of things happening without their knowledge. Probably there will not be much time for the topic to be developed very far, as this assembly will usually be the first one in the spring term. However, the teacher should discuss the theme with the children before introducing it at the assembly.

If possible, take the children into a garden, or ask them to look at their own garden at home, especially at the earth. Let them feel it — cold, damp and hard. What could possibly be happening there? Let them look at the bare branches of the trees and let them handle the apparently dead twigs. Something secret is happening within them. Show pictures of spring flowers, trees in full leaf, and green fields, so that they can wonder at the growth going on under and above the earth. It may be difficult for very young children to appreciate the concept that God is providing for us, year after year: seeds will germinate, trees will produce fruit, and animals will multiply.

The boys and girls may have heard of New Year resolutions, but few will have made any. The idea of making one, and keeping it a secret so that it grows into something good, quietly and without being noticed, might appeal to them. Pictures of children at different stages of growth, growth that is unnoticed by themselves, alongside pictures of the seed growing into the flower, might help, and could certainly be shown at the assembly.

If there are many immigrant children attending the assembly, remember that nearly every religion celebrates a New Year, albeit at different times. It is worth finding out something about the celebrations of Jews, Hindus, Sikhs and Muslims. A mobile of symbols connected with these religions could be made, or a large hanging cube of pictures showing them could be constructed.

The assembly

Hymns and songs

God, who made the earth	NCS 6
In the winter, birds need food	NCS 26
We thank you, loving Father God	NCS 27
All the flowers are sleeping	SSL 48, verse 4

Poem

Ready for spring

Working in secret, a little brown bulb
   Pushed through the earth one day,
First its green shoot looked round at the world,
   And here's what it seemed to say,
'It's cold and damp, and rather dark,
   I'm too little to see the sky,
If I push and push, I'll grow some more,
   It's hard by myself, but I'll try!'
Down came the rain, then the sun came through;
   'We'll help,' they both tried to say,
'You've a force within you that's healthy and strong,
   And you'll bloom as a flower one day.'
Silently, slowly, the little bulb worked,
   Helped by the sun and the rain,
Until it was tall, with a lovely bright flower,
   Ready for spring again.

Music
  Little Bells from *Wand of Youth Suite No 2*, Elgar

Prayer
  O God, we love secret things; thank you for the way you work in seeds and bulbs and the sleeping trees. When we look round in the springtime at the new flowers and the green leaves, help us to remember what you have been doing for us all the winter.

Stories

Bible stories: The creation of the world — selected from Genesis 1.1 to 2.4
Parables of the mustard seed and the yeast —
Matthew 13.31-33
Secret things (told in full)

Secret things

Daddy said that Hamish was to go on holiday for a week or two. Hamish had had chicken-pox at Christmas, and it hadn't been a very happy time. Mummy had wanted to look after him, but she was going to have a new baby and the doctor had asked her to rest a lot. Daddy had been very good, though, dabbing lotion on Hamish's itchy spots, and reading stories to him. Auntie Margaret had written when she knew about Hamish's chicken-pox and asked if he would like to go to stay with her for the New Year. Auntie Margaret and Uncle John had a farm in the country. Hamish wondered what there would be to do on a farm in the middle of winter.

'Can I watch the cows being milked?' he asked Uncle John as soon as he arrived. Uncle John said he would have to get up very early in the morning to see that happening. It was so cold the next morning that Hamish decided to stay in bed instead!

Later, he watched Auntie Margaret making bread and cakes and she let him scrape round the bowl when she had creamed the cake mixture. But she wouldn't let him touch the bread dough which she left standing on top of the warm oven. 'Come back and look at it with me in an hour,' she said to Hamish. He thought it sounded rather a dull thing to do, but in an hour his aunt reminded him about it. He looked at the bread dough. It had grown! When she left it on the oven it had been quite small, now it was almost the size of a football!

'Coo!' said Hamish. 'How did that happen?'

Auntie Margaret told him that she had put yeast into the mixture. When it was left in a warm place, the yeast made the dough swell and rise, to make it ready for baking into the lovely bread he enjoyed eating at teatime. 'It works secretly,' she told him.

Later, Uncle John came in, tired and hungry.

'What is there to do on a farm in January?' asked Hamish.

'Oh, lots of things!' said his uncle. 'All sorts of things are happening and working in secret. Come and see a secret I've got in the barn.'

Hamish put on his warm coat and his woolly hat and his wellington boots. Uncle took him across the muddy yard and past the milking sheds, to the big warm barn. In a corner stood one of the sheep from the field. And beside her,

51

lying in the hay, was a little white new-born lamb. Hamish was quiet, and he moved very slowly, so that the lamb wouldn't be frightened. 'What a lovely secret!' he said as they left, closing the big doors carefully.

On the way back to the farmhouse Uncle John showed Hamish something else that had happened secretly: a tiny snowdrop, white and sturdy, had grown from a little brown bulb, right by the garden fence. 'There will be more here soon,' said Uncle John, pointing to the thin green leaves of the snowdrop plants.

At the end of two weeks Daddy and Mummy came to fetch Hamish by car. They were going back to their own home. Hamish rushed out to meet the car when he saw it arrive. Daddy got out and hugged him.

'There's a secret in the car,' said Daddy. 'Go and ask Mummy what it is.'

Hamish rushed to the front of the car. Mummy opened the door and Hamish climbed on to her lap.

'Look on the back seat, Hamish,' she said. Hamish looked behind him. There, in a carrycot, was the secret — their new baby. 'It's a little girl,' said Mummy. 'We're calling her Amy.'

Hamish loved secrets, and this was the best one of all. And it was such fun to be going home.

Snow and ice

Project outline

In many parts of this country falls of snow are infrequent and short-lived. A project such as this may therefore have to be speedily prepared, and adapted to last as long as the weather. When the snow has turned to brown slush, and the icicles dripped out of existence, the children's excitement and pleasure will also have waned, a poor time for any project. But the sight of a white world and the muffled sound of traffic in a usually noisy neighbourhood is thrilling to a young child. By the time the boys and girls arrive in the class-room on such a morning, they will have stamped on the snow, held it in their hands, been chilled by it, and will probably have tasted it. Once in the warm class-room they will be ready to talk about it, and be receptive and responsible, especially if the teacher is also prepared.

The colour of God's world should be noted, in pictures using white chalk or paint on black paper, or in words of wonder in poems and descriptive writings. Do not neglect feelings and emotions, though; let the children analyse, as far as they are able, how they first felt when they saw the snow, touched it, played with it, or walked through it. Have ready large pictures of snowflake patterns, many different ones, emphasising the very special significance of God's attention to detail. The children will enjoy cutting or tearing out six-sided snowflake patterns, and sticking them on blue paper, either in a geometric formation or in a haphazard montage. These can be shown at the assembly.

Talk to the children about countries where snow is thick and long-lasting, and about how people living there adapt to the conditions, in the way they heat their homes, travel, communicate, and enjoy themselves — skiing, tobogganing, etc. Show pictures of snow-ploughs, and of farmers being particularly careful of their animals, giving them extra food and shelter, and searching for any that have become stranded or buried in the snow.

Looking for secret signs — tracks of animals, birds, vehicles or people — can be an interesting piece of detective work for children living in either the town or the country. Some teachers will be able to take their class to search for such signs, coming back into the class-room to record and discuss the findings. Others should provide pictures and photographs, and encourage the children to look for their own signs. Be aware of what television and radio presenters are likely to do; they are quick to use the changing weather in their factual and finding-out programmes.

Build up a frieze for the class-room and for display at the assembly. Use white paper mounted on deep yellow or blue, in the shape of hills and foreground. Adapt the frieze to fit the situation of the school: town or country, isolated or built-up area, and so on. Many things can be put on it (use the children's unaided work where possible): houses and cars with snow-covered roofs; children, warmly wrapped, playing in the snow, on slides, swings, toboggans; shepherds looking for their sheep; farmers putting hay in the fields for their cattle; men clearing snow in the main roads; and people using sand and salt on doorsteps (a useful and interesting experiment in itself). Animal and bird tracks can be added to the scene by the children making their own 'stamps' from potato cuts or from drinking straws glued to wood blocks, or stencils cut from card; make use, too, of sponges, corks, cut paper and many discarded materials, all of which could add to the freshness and excitement of the frieze.

At the end of this time the snow will probably be disappearing or have gone, but in prolonged wintry conditions there is still much work that could be done. Discoveries about Eskimos and their igloos; arctic and antarctic animals and explorations; the properties of ice and experiments with it; or animal hibernation.

Ideally, the children will have seen the wonder of God in the snow, in its vastness and in its detail. The teacher, mindful of the opportunities for using this sense of wonder in an assembly, will have related the children's discoveries and excitement to God who has made them possible.

The assembly

Hymns and songs

We thank you, loving Father God	NCS 27	
See how the snowflakes are falling	NCS 28	SSL 57
To God who makes all lovely things	SSL 9	
Little birds in winter time	SSL 43	

Music

    Overture: Land of the Mountains and the Flood, Hamish MacCunn
    (Make use of the main theme following the opening introduction)
    In the hall of the Mountain King from *Peer Gynt Suite,* Grieg

Poem

Snowy morning

Low,
bending low
under the snow,
the branch
of the tree
touches the ground
where the grass
used to be.

God,
Father God —
look where he trod,
changing
the green
of yesterday's grass —
you can see
where he's been.

White,
paper white
an unreal light;
the cat
picks her way
lifting her paws
to shake off
cold spray.

White,
paper white,
the morning light
sparkles
with sunshine,
touching the world,
making it
diamond-fine.

Prayer

Thank you, dear God, for all kinds of fun, especially the fun we can have in the snow and on the ice. Help us to see how beautiful your world looks at this time of year.

Stories

Bible verses: Readings of Job 37.2-6, 9-12; and Psalm 147.15-18
The enchanted bedroom (told in full)

The enchanted bedroom

Bindu used to live in a very hot country called Uganda in the middle of Africa. Her mother and father and many other Asian families were leaving Africa at the very hottest time of the year to go to live in England. Bindu was excited when they walked up the steps to the plane at the airport. In the aeroplane she tried to look out through the little windows to see the land below. Mother and Father talked together about England and about Uncle Bhavneet who had gone on ahead to find a house for them all. Bindu remembered the day the letter had come from him, telling them about the house that he had bought. It was in a town called Bradford. He said that he was decorating a little bedroom in it specially for Bindu. Her bedroom in the house they had lived in in Kampala had been big and rather bare, and the sun had shone in through the window every day.

Father said that England was sometimes very cold, but Bindu couldn't imagine it. As the plane landed, it was beginning to get dark, and Bindu shivered. Mother pulled a rug round her, and put on a thick coat herself. Bindu was nearly asleep. She heard Uncle Bhavneet's voice as he came forward from the crowd to greet them.

'I've got a car waiting,' he said. 'The house is quite a long way from the airport. We shan't be there until about 11 o'clock.'

Bindu tried to stay awake and look out of the window. England was quite different from Uganda; and it was so cold. She huddled further into the rug on the back seat.

'There's a little bedroom for Bindu,' Uncle Bhavneet was saying. 'Just room for a bed and a chest of drawers. We've put up blue curtains at the windows.'

'What can I see from the window?' asked Bindu, sleepily.

'Lots of rooftops and chimneys,' said Uncle Bhavneet.

That sounded horrid, thought Bindu as she fell asleep. She began to dream. She dreamt she was in a small bed in a enchanted bedroom — a bedroom fit for an Indian princess, silver and blue and richly patterned. 'It's beautiful, so beautiful,' she sighed.

The car had stopped, but Bindu kept her eyes shut. She was so tired that she didn't really mind what the street in Bradford looked like, or the house where she was to live. She would see it all in the morning. It was so cold, too! She wondered if the big golden sun ever shone in England.

Uncle Bhavneet wrapped her more tightly in the rug and carried her gently through the front door and up the stairs. She was almost asleep when he laid her on her own little bed.

'Is it like a princess' bedroom?' asked Bindu, with her eyes shut.

'Wait till you wake up in the morning,' said Uncle Bhavneet. 'It might be.'

Next time Bindu opened her eyes it was morning, and the light was shining in through the blue curtains at the window. The whole room looked pale blue and beautiful. There were blue roses on the wallpaper, too.

Bindu gasped. 'A princess' bedroom,' she whispered. She still had the rug wrapped tightly round her. It was much colder than she had thought it would be. For a little while she lay snuggled in her bed pretending to be a princess, dressed in blue and silver. She was a princess in her little blue room, like a cave of blue light, full of flowers and jewels.

'Come along, Bindu,' said Mother, opening the bedroom door. 'It's time you were up. Look at this lovely thick jumper Uncle Bhavneet has bought for you. It will keep you really warm.' She put it on the end of the bed and went to the window.

'Don't push the curtains back,' said Bindu quickly, afraid that her beautiful royal bedroom would be spoilt. She didn't want to see the grey rooftops and the chimneys.

But Mother had already pulled back the curtains and let in the light. Bindu stared at the window. She had expected to see row upon row of houses with tall grey roofs. Instead, there was the most beautiful pattern of silver leaves and ferns all over the windows. Her little room was silver and blue and patterned just as she had imagined it.

'Where are the houses and the rooftops?' Bindu asked, really glad that, just at the moment, she couldn't see them.

'Uncle Bhavneet says it's so cold that the frost has patterned the windows with ice,' Mother said.

Suddenly, Bindu loved England, with its cold weather and its rooftops and its smoky chimneys. It was just as beautiful in her little bedroom as it had been anywhere in Africa, and she really did feel like a princess.

Happiness

Project outline

The long days of winter often produce long faces. Christmas has gone, taking with it the happy spirit of goodwill and feelings of wellbeing and warmth. How pleasant to meet, at this time, a person who can bring back that warmth with his or her sense of humour, happy smile or cheery greeting!

Begin the preparations for this assembly by doing something with the children that they enjoy — a party game, or a treat of orange juice and a biscuit, or a progressive games afternoon, or by telling a well-known and often-asked-for story. Afterwards talk to the children about how they felt: did they have a happy feeling? Go back to this theme the following day, and remind them again of what happened. Do they still feel happy when they think about it? Talk about the coming assembly and its theme of happiness.

Find out how much they can remember of Christmas. (If there are immigrants in the class, concentrate on the school celebrations, as these may be all that they experienced.) What were their feelings at Christmas time? Some might be able to write about them, others to draw or paint aspects of Christmas that particularly pleased them. What made Christmas fun? The excitement of anticipation, fed by the sight of decorations, shop displays, wrapping paper, cards, school entertainments, carols etc. How could we make the school happy now? Put some quickly-made decorations in the hall; make cards for each of the other classes and for the staff, with the words 'Happy February' (or whatever month it is) on them. A large banner with the same words would create some excitement at the assembly. If a bowl of daffodils or other flowers is available, this should be on show. These are a promise of happy times when spring comes. One way of making people happy, the children will realise, is by stirring up excitement in them by pleasant words, greetings, and showing happy pictures.

Now the teacher should seek to find out what else makes the children happy. A list should be compiled from their suggestions, with things such as games, food, mothers and fathers, outings, treats and jokes. Young children love jokes, even when they don't quite understand them! Tell some jokes, and ask the class to notice how telling them alters the faces of the audience. One or two selected jokes could be told to the rest of the school at the assembly;

make sure they are told by a child who can speak slowly and clearly, or there will be little response at all. Another way of altering people's expressions is to smile at them. Few people can resist smiling in return. Tell the children to try smiling at people they know and frequently meet: shop-keepers, teachers, dinner ladies, the crossing attendant on the street corner, and so on. (Be cautious about encouraging them to smile at strangers, though.) Tell them to watch the people's faces change as they respond. Making people happy is also an interaction of facial expressions.

Lastly, happiness can be spread by doing things: making other people happy by helping, making, serving, giving, etc. Talk with the children about this, and act scenes of happiness-spreading, eg, Grandma goes to get out of her chair; Johnnie asks what she wants and goes fetch it; Grandma is pleased and happy. How does she show it?

To use the given poem effectively, each child will need to make two paper faces from circles about 24cm in diameter. On one the child should portray a sad face, with the eyebrows drawn together in a frown, and the mouth turned down, and on the other a happy face, with a broad smile. (Encourage them to copy each other's appropriate facial expressions.) These faces could be completed with paint, sticky paper or with the addition of pipe cleaners, wool and buttons. These circular faces should then be stuck, back to back, with a length of wood or rolled-up newspaper between them to act as a holder. During the first verse of the poem the sad face should be held up, mask-like, in front of the child's face. In the second verse the mask should be reversed.

The assembly

Hymns and songs

Clap-a-your hands, sing-a-for joy	NCS 58
Let's beat a song of praise	NCS 71
O Lord! Shout for joy	SSL 4
Stand up, clap hands	SSL 14

Poem

Faces

Look at us all with our sad, sorry faces,
    Each with a scowl and a frown;
See how our eyes have no merry twinkle,
    And our mouths are all turning down.

But look how we've changed in one little minute!
We're smiling and laughing for you;
And when you see how our mouths have turned up
We're sure you'll feel happiness too!

Music

Waltz from *Suite 116,* Godard
(Jolly, happy music introducing the solo flute)
Jesu, joy of man's desiring or
Sheep may safely graze, Bach
(Use the piano transcription to convey the sense of calm, inward happiness)

Prayer

Father God, help us always to wear a happy smile, so that other people can
see us and feel happy.

Stories

Bible stories: The lost sheep — Luke 15.4-7
The lost piece of silver — Luke 15.8-10
Making Mother happy (told in ful)

Making Mother happy

Ghezala hadn't been in England very long. Father had brought the family
over from Pakistan so that they could join Uncle Nazar in Birmingham.
Uncle Nazar said England was a good place in which to live. Ghezala and her
family arrived just after Christmas. They had left Pakistan on a very hot day,
and Uncle Nazar had met them at the airport with warm coats.

Ghezala rushed about looking at things in her new home. Everything was
so different from her home in Kallat. There it had been hot and dry and
dusty, and the houses were made of white stone, and the front door opened
straight on to the road. Here the houses were very close together, but they did
have small gardens. Their garden was very overgrown, but Father and Uncle
Nazar had plans for growing vegetables later on when the weather was
warmer. Ghezala also wanted to explore the part of Birmingham where she
lived. Having so many shops and so much to choose from was exciting, and
many of the people looked friendly. But most of all she wanted to go on the
common. She had seen it when Uncle brought them home from the airport.
It stretched green and bushy across a huge area not far from her home.

It took a long time, weeks after Ghezala had begun at her new school, to
persuade Mother to go out of the front door. Mother missed her old friends,

and she was frightened to go to the shops, and most of all she was cold, so cold she didn't think she would ever be warm again. Sometimes she cried when she thought of Pakistan and all she had had to leave behind.

One day Father came home from work with a friend. 'Mr Ali will take us to the common in his car,' he told Ghezala. 'Tell Mother to put on her warmest clothes.'

But Mother didn't look happy, even when she heard about the visit to the common. Ghezala did want to see her smile again.

Mr Ali parked the car on the edge of the common, and they all got out.

'Hurrah!' shouted Ghezala, and leapt ahead. 'Can we walk this way?'

Mother and Father and Mr Ali followed slowly. Mother held her coat tightly over her sari. 'I think I'll go back and sit in the car,' she said.

'No, Mother, do come with us,' said Ghezala. She had stopped running and told the others to stand still. 'Listen!' she said. A sweet singing sound could be heard: it was a blackbird, singing happily on a tree nearby.

'Isn't that lovely?' she asked. Mother turned her head slightly, and then they went on walking.

'Look! A pond!' said Ghezala.

'It smells,' said Mother.

'But look down there,' said Ghezala. 'I can see frogspawn. We've got some in a jar at school. It will turn into tadpoles and then into frogs.'

Mother turned to look at the spotty jelly. She almost smiled, but then they walked on. Soon they came to an open part of the common.

'Look!' said Ghezala again.

'Oh,' said Mother. 'How awful! People have been bringing all their rubbish and dumping it on the common! I'm going back!'

'Oh, Mother,' said Ghezala. 'You're looking at all the wrong things.' Ghezala had seen some little yellow flowers, peeping out from under some of the rubbish. She picked one, and then another, and then another. Soon she had a little bunch of the bright celandines.

'They're for you,' she said, giving them to her mother.

'Thank you,' said Mother. At last she looked really happy. 'You know, Ghezala, I think I *have* been looking at all the wrong things, ever since we came to England. If I'm going to be happy here I've got to learn to see the right things all the time.'

Ghezala was glad too; now Mother would settle down and be happy in this country. She was smiling and looking happily about her for the first time since they had arrived. And she hadn't even noticed that her beautiful sari was trailing in the mud!

Families

Project outline

In Infant schools it is often possible for the teacher to know a fair amount about the families and homes from which the children in her class come. The normal outgoing boy or girl of 5-7 will often confide more intimate details about the happenings at home than their parents would wish! From these snatches of conversation and pieces of written 'news' the teacher will build her own picture of the family. She will also usually have ample opportunity for contact with the parents and will know of any problems and family difficulties the children or their near relatives have to face. Often, to the teacher's eyes, these are considerable. For example, two small children, barely old enough for school, known to the writer of this book, had to remain in the house alone after their parents had gone to work early in the morning, cook their own breakfast, and wait for a phone call from their father to tell them when to leave the house to go to school. Another small boy, because he would not wash or brush his own hair (at only five years old), had to suffer the humiliation of having his head shaved by his own father. Imagine the ridicule this aroused in the school playground! So the teacher should never assume that the children in her class come from idyllic, secure families. Most of them, however, will have some degree of a warm relationship with a mother or father, and many of them with both.

The project for this theme would probably be best built up by looking at other families — perhaps using a bird family as the main subject. The courting, mating and nesting; the hatching of eggs and the subsequent feeding, care and protection of the young, make a sound basis for this topic. If possible, study a common garden bird or, if the time of year is right, it might be possible to have an actual nest known to the children as a starting point.

A visit to a zoo, or an aviary, or some nesting budgerigars, could also provide a talking point, or a motivation for the project. Diaries, models, writings, drawings and research could all become part of it, leaving the teacher with much display material for the assembly, and the children with a good basic interest in ornithology.

If, however, the class has a special interest in hamsters, gerbils or rabbits, with easy access to a breeding group, the project should centre round the care and protection of their young, and the preparations made by the parents for them. Similarly, if the children know any dogs or cats who happen to be producing puppies or kittens, these should be talked about and perhaps brought into the class-room. Older Infants can do some delightful pieces of creative writing about animals and birds, and many of the pictures they do are worth preserving. These writings and pictures should be shown or talked about at the assembly.

The assembly

Hymns and songs

At half past three we go home to tea	NCS 43	SSL 58
When Jesus was a little boy	NCS 57	
Mummy does the shopping	NCS 95	
It fell upon a summer day	SSL 31	

Poem

The bird mother

What can you see as you sit in the tree
    Singing so loud and so long?
The little bird mother, she looked at me
    From up in her tree,
And she went on singing her song.

Where is your nest, little mother bird,
    Is it some way away?
She answered me with a few bright words
    (That I'm sure I heard),
'If you follow I'll show the way.'

She flew to the hedge by the garden wall,
    I peeped through the leaves to see;
She stood by her nest, so proud, so tall,
    By her chicks so small,
Protecting her babies from me.

'You may look at my nest, you may hear me,
    But leave me in peace, I pray;
Don't make a loud noise when you're near me,
    Try not to scare me,
I'm protecting my young today.'

Prayer

Thank you, Father God, for mothers and fathers and friends; for all the people who make us comfortable, who feed us, and make us happy. Thank you for our brothers and sisters. Make us all glad to be together. Help us to be one happy family at school, too.

Stories

Bible stories: The father who loved his son — Luke 15.11-24
            Jesus at a happy wedding feast — John 2.1-10
Miranda's family (told in full)

Miranda's family

Pat, who lived in the next flat to Miranda, had had a baby brother. Miranda had been in to see him as soon as she could; she thought Pat was so lucky — she had a real baby to help to look after. Pat said that her mother had let her tuck the baby into his carrycot, and she was allowed to rock him gently when he cried. Pat's mother said that Miranda could hold the baby, if she sat on the settee and kept very still. Miranda's mother sat there too, just in case he got too heavy.

Miranda looked at the baby boy. He was asleep, his little face all screwed up and wrinkled. 'When will he be big enough to play with?' she asked.

Pat said, 'Oh, not for ages; Mummy told me he won't be able to do anything but eat and sleep for a long time.'

Miranda wanted a little brother, too. She had wanted someone else to play with for a long time. It was all right playing with the boys and girls in the flats, and it was fun when she met them in the play area far below her balcony. But she wanted her own brother, someone to share her secrets with, someone to laugh with under cover of the bedclothes, someone to eat breakfast with. She always had to say goodbye to the other children at teatime.

'I want a brother,' she said every morning when she woke up.

One day, as she and Mummy and Daddy walked along a wide road in their town, Miranda noticed a big house behind some tall trees.

'What's in there?' she asked.

'Boys and girls,' said Daddy. 'It's a children's home.'

'How many live there?' asked Miranda.

'Eight, I think; maybe more,' said Daddy.

All those boys and girls together, thought Miranda. Actually living together all day and every day. What fun they must have!

'The children who live there have no proper homes,' explained Mummy.

'They could come and live with us,' said Miranda. 'We've got a proper home.'

'Perhaps we could visit one of the little boys,' said Daddy, looking across at Mummy. 'Let's think about it when we get home.'

As they got lunch ready Mummy said that perhaps one of the little boys at the home would like to come to tea sometimes. 'We'll go and see the house mother,' she said.

She and Daddy made lots of phone calls, and a week or so later, someone came to see them. She told them that there was a little boy in the home called Timothy, who very badly wanted someone to love.

'We'll visit him on Saturday,' said Daddy.

Timothy was only three, and was a bit shy. He wouldn't talk to Mummy and Daddy at first, but he took Miranda's hand and showed her where the cat went to sleep, and where he kept his very own teddy bear.

They went to see Timothy often, and he looked forward to their visits. One day the house mother said she thought he was ready to go to tea with them in their flat. Miranda enjoyed that; it was a pity he had to go back to the home when it was time for bed. She wished she had Timothy for a brother, and she was sure he wanted her for a sister.

A month later Timothy went to stay with them for a weekend. He laughed when Mummy bathed him, and Miranda gave him her favourite bath boat. She tucked him up in a little bed in the corner of her room, and showed him her best story book with the pop-up pictures.

Timothy fitted in with the family very well and almost cried when he had to go back to the big house behind the tall trees.

'When can I come to stay again?' he asked.

After that he came often, until the people at the children's home felt that he was quite ready to go and live with them for a very long time, maybe for always. Miranda was so happy: now she had her own brother, one who could already talk and run and play. That night she told him all her secrets, and they laughed together under cover of the bedclothes.

Spring

Project outline

Taken not too early in the year, a project and assembly about spring can be full of meaning for young children. They can experience just as deeply as adults the joy of returning life. But adults have had many years of annual anticipation, and so are often immune to the surprise of spring. The teacher's aim should be first to feel again the hope-laden atmosphere around her, and then to transmit this perception to her children.

Sleeping, seemingly dead and unattractive things could be the starting point. Show some of autumn's bulbs, twigs with buds which still look lifeless, perhaps the chrysalis of a moth or butterfly hidden for the winter in the peeling bark of a tree or, if possible, a hibernating tortoise.

Make a class-room picture of a bare winter tree on blue paper; as the days pass, the children should make bright green paper leaves, and stick a few leaves on each day until, by the assembly, the tree will be covered in bright spring foliage. Or a more slender tree with less foliage could be made, and pink or white tissue-paper flowers added. Chestnut (sticky) buds brought into the class-room will open fairly quickly in the warm atmosphere; and other buds similarly. Bulbs that have already begun to open in the class-room could be drawn in a sequence of pictures — records may have been kept since the time of planting, and these will be useful now. Use these for display, and pictures from seed and gardening catalogues. In addition, the teacher could organise the planting, and subsequent watering, watching and recording of mustard and cress seeds, or bean shoot seeds. The children will see easily and quickly that apparently useless seeds will burst into life given the right care and conditions. Carrot tops will also flourish if stood in a saucer of water for a week or so.

In spring, then, God creates the conditions of extra warmth, and the stimulus of sunshine and longer daylight hours. Man provides much of the care. Talk about the farmers, and how they prepared the ground ready for the seeds. They are already looking ahead to the time of harvest. They are caring for their animals, too, who are producing new life: calves, lambs and chicks. Drawings, cut-outs, friezes, of all these could be made and commented upon.

The children will enjoy watching tadpoles emerge from frogspawn — very much a spring happening; the teacher can enlarge the topic with stories and poems of hibernating animals waking up, birds building nests and laying eggs, and mother hens and ducks protecting their newly-hatched young.

Spring, too, is looked upon as a time when people renew, repair and refresh, preparing for the summer months. Landladies redecorate ready for summer visitors, mothers do the spring cleaning, washing away the winter dirt, and fathers begin cutting the lawn as the new growth of grass appears. The children could write about and illustrate any of these happenings that they have seen.

The assembly

Hymns and songs

Sing a song of May-time	NCS 14
What is the west wind singing	NCS 17
Morning has broken	SSL 3
All the flowers are waking	SSL 48

Poem

Spring things

Can you see the signs of spring
   As you walk along the lane?
The lambs are with their mothers,
   And the cuckoo's back again.

Can you see the signs of spring
   As you walk about the town?
The pigeons are nesting in the eaves
   And the avenue's green, not brown.

Can you see the signs of spring
   As you walk through your front door?
Mother's getting the curtains down
   And washing them all once more.

Look for the signs of spring today
   In the home or town or lane,
The winter of yesterday's almost gone,
   And there's plenty of life again.

Music
   Song without words No 30: Spring Song, Mendelssohn
   Slow movement from *Symphony No 1 (Spring),* Schumann

Prayer
   Looking at spring blossom, or pictures of lambs, etc
   Dear God, we can see the signs of spring all round us; thank you for them.
   This is a lovely time of year; help us to be happy in it.

Stories
   Bible stories: A simplified reading of Psalm 104.10-12
                  The sower — Luke 8.4-8
   The dragon of the deep (told in full)

The dragon of the deep

There was once a dragon, brown and nasty looking. To Terence the tadpole
he was huge and horrible. The dragon lived at the bottom of Terence's pond,
but he was hidden in the mud most of the time. Terence and his brother
tadpoles sometimes swam too near his hiding place and were terribly
frightened when he swam towards them, twirling the mud into dark,
brownish mist. He snapped his great jaws at them in warning. 'If you come
too close I shall eat you,' he growled.

Terence spoke to the old water beetle. 'He wasn't here last summer,' said
the beetle, who knew the creatures in the pond very well. 'And now here he is,
terrorising everyone.' He told Terence how several small unsuspecting
creatures had been snapped up in the dragon's jaws and eaten. 'Keep well
away from him,' said the water beetle. 'He'll never be any good.'

So Terence kept well away, hiding behind the plants that grew in the
water. He played with the strings of toad-spawn, and sometimes he rose to
the surface of the pond to talk to his friends the water-boatmen who skated
over the water. Some days the water was clear and warm, and on other days
raindrops from the sky fell making big patterns on the surface.

As time went on Terence grew some back legs. 'What's happening to me?'
he asked the old water beetle.

'It happens to all tadpoles,' said the beetle. 'You won't always live in the
water, swimming about among the plants and playing with your friends.'

'Where will I go? What will become of me?' asked Terence.

'You will grow four legs and lose that tail of yours,' said the old water
beetle. 'Then you will jump out of the water.'

'Out on to all that dry land?' asked Terence. He couldn't imagine what it would be like.

'You will be a frog then,' the water beetle was saying. 'You will grow big and strong. And next spring you will come back to the pond again.'

Terence wanted to grow up quickly. If he was big and strong he wouldn't be afraid of the brown dragon.

A week or two later Terence had his front legs too, and his tail began to get smaller. He went up to talk to the water-boatmen more often, because he liked gulping in the fresh air from above the water.

He still kept well away from the dragon. He had heard that small frogs weren't very safe from his jaws. Often he teased the dragon by sitting on a rock near the surface of the water and waiting until he appeared. Just as the dragon began snapping hungrily at Terence, the little frog would do a huge jump and land a long way away.

One day the ugly dragon wasn't in any of his usual spots, waiting to eat small creatures that went by. Terence looked all round the pond and at last he saw him, slowly climbing up the stalk of one of the tall water plants. He called to him cheekily, but the dragon took no notice.

'You're nearly at the top of the water,' shouted Terence. 'You'd better get back quickly!' But the dragon went on climbing. He was even more ugly as he climbed. Terence was afraid that he, too, was going to live on the land. 'Whatever shall I do then?' he asked himself.

When he was a little way out of the water the dragon stopped climbing and clung to the plant, quite still.

'He's fallen asleep,' thought Terence, and jumped right out of the water to see what would happen.

Then the dragon began to change, very slowly, as Terence watched. A large crack opened all down his back. Something was coming out of the crack — a head, and a body, and legs, and then a long, long tail. And wings, too, that the dragon (or whatever it had become) stretched and dried in the sunshine. Its body and tail were a beautiful blue, shining and quivering, long and delicate. Terence couldn't believe it. The nasty brown dragon had changed into this magnificent creature.

At that moment the dragon-fly, which was what the dragon had become, shook its wings, waved its feelers, and left its leaf. It flew over the surface of the pond, darting and hovering.

Terence followed it for a minute or two, jumping and croaking like a grown-up frog. He was glad the dragon wasn't a dragon any more.

(It will be helpful and effective if, as she tells the story, the teacher shows pictures of the various water creatures mentioned.)

Our eyes

Project outline

An item of the children's news, or some random conversation, could give a lead into this topic. Watch out for the movement when sight or seeing is talked about, or when eyes become the pivot of attention, and use this time to open out the thinking.

Differences in the colour, shape and size of eyes amongst the class members should be noted and graphs made. This should lead to discussions about the iris, the colour, size and shape at various times, and how this depends on the amount of light passing through it. The children will enjoy noticing this and recording it in words and pictures.

Carry out experiments so that the children become aware of their own eyes: their range of vision and their ability to make judgements of distance and size. Older children will be fascinated by illusions and how eyes can often play visual tricks. They can do experiments that will contradict the adage 'seeing is believing'; eg, by looking through a long cardboard roll with one eye, and by moving one's hand, palm facing the other eye (which remains open), along the roll, it would appear that the moving hand has a hole through its centre!

Further work could include discussions and discoveries about animal and insect camouflage, the use of X-rays, mirrors, periscopes and kaleidoscopes, or light itself in its many forms, or magazine illustrations, photographs, cartoons and moving pictures.

Most Infant school children will be able to recall having their eyes tested; this should be talked about. Children already wearing glasses will become important, and those waiting for glasses, or newly fitted with them, will be helped over what is often a traumatic time. Other aids to seeing should be included here — magnifying glasses, telescopes and microscopes, etc. If these could be shown to and used by the children, it would add greatly to their understanding of improving sight.

Any recorded work, written or illustrated, should be displayed at the assembly; those with glasses might tell about their particular eye tests or fitting for spectacles. Any available instruments such as microscopes or binoculars should be shown to the school. Simple periscopes and prisms might be made, spectrums coloured, and patterns from kaleidoscopes enlarged. Activity and display material for the topic seem endless; the teacher's problem will probably be one of selection and elimination!

The assembly

Hymns and songs

Look up! Look up!	NCS 1
What do we see on a warm spring day?	NCS 18
Give to us eyes	SSL 18
Praise to God for things we see	SSL 20

Poem

I spy ...

I spy with my little eye —
   What can I spy today?
The clouds that sail in the big blue sky,
The buses and lorries that pass me by,
The birds in the hedge and the little black fly,
   These I can spy today.

I spy an ice-cream man
   As I go out to play,
And the man who sweeps the path so well,
The bus-conductor who rings the bell,
And the lady who picked me up when I fell,
   I can see them all today.

I spy all sorts of things,
   People and animals too,
Thank God for my eyes this lovely day:
I can read and write, I can work and play,
I can see my friends when they smile and say,
   'I'm glad to be friends with you!'

Prayer

For this prayer suggest that the children keep their eyes open, fixed on a vase of flowers, a colourful picture, or a window with a view.

As we look at your beautiful world, Father God, we praise you. We thank you for our eyes, and for being able to see pictures and words, movement and colour. We thank you, too, for the people who make spectacles and magnifying glasses, telescopes and microscopes, so that we may see your world more clearly. We know there are some people who cannot see at all. Help them to discover your wonderful world in other ways.

Stories
Bible stories: God saw that it was good — Genesis 1.1 to 2.4
The blind man at Bethsaida — Mark 8.22-25
Magic glass (told in full)

Magic glass

The school nurse had suggested that Chris should wear glasses, and the eye-doctor had agreed. Chris and his mother had chosen a smart pair of frames into which his own special lenses would be fitted. There was even a red leather case to keep them in at night time. 'Wait until you get home, and then put them on,' said the eye-doctor. 'They will seem strange at first, and you'll have to get used to them.'

Chris looked in the mirror when he put the glasses on at home. He thought he really looked quite handsome. He would wear them at school tomorrow and everyone would admire them.

But it wasn't like that at all. On the way to school he met Claire Jones. 'You do look funny,' she said. 'You've got glasses on!'

Of course, Claire was only a girl, and girls weren't very sensible. They didn't ever see things like boys did. Chris was sure the boys would notice how handsome the glasses made him look. At the school gate stood Robert Martin. He stared at Chris. Then he laughed. 'Got to wear glasses?' he asked. 'You won't be able to play football, you know!'

'Look at Chris!' said another boy. 'You got to wear those all day?'

Chris began to think that perhaps he didn't look handsome after all. 'Course not!' he said. 'I've got a case here to put them in. Just thought I'd show you what they looked like. They're not much good, really.' He took them off and put them into the red leather case. It was quite surprising how blurred everything looked without them on. He felt very miserable. Today wasn't turning out at all well. Just then the whistle went and all the boys and girls hurried to their class-rooms. Chris sat at his table quickly and started looking at a book.

'Why, Chris!' said Miss Mackirk. 'Your mother told me you'd be wearing glasses today. I was looking forward to seeing them!'

. Chris glared at her. 'I haven't really got to wear them,' he said, screwing up his eyes as he tried to see her clearly.

'Just show them to me then,' said Miss Mackirk kindly. Chris took the red leather case out of his pocket and handed it to his teacher. He hoped she wouldn't ask him to put them on. 'Now they're really smart!' she said. 'Aren't you lucky?'

Later that morning, Miss Mackirk opened the big cupboard in the classroom. She took three things out of it.

'This is a telescope,' she said, holding up a long metal tube. 'When you look in at this end you look through some bits of glass — magic glass — that help you to see much further than you could with just your own eyes. Sometimes telescopes are so enormous and the magic glass is so powerful that you can see craters on the moon quite clearly. And your eyesight can be stretched to see stars that are usually invisible.'

Chris had seen pictures of them. He knew that men had had to study the moon through telescopes very carefully before sending up astronauts to land on it.

Miss Mackirk held up the second object. 'These are binoculars,' she said. 'They are made with two shorter tubes. They make things in the distance seem very much nearer when you look through them. We'll take them into the playground later on and you can see for yourselves.'

The last thing she held up was like a miniature telescope on a little stand. One by one the children were allowed to go and look through it at a tiny bubble of water that had been caught between two pieces of glass. Chris put his eye to it. He could see things moving — swimming. He took his eye away and looked at the water on the plate. It looked completely empty and clear. When he looked through the tube again, there they were once more, little creatures wriggling and moving.

'This is a microscope,' Miss Mackirk was saying. 'We use it to see very small things more clearly. The magic glass in the tube makes tiny things seem much bigger. Aren't we lucky that, long ago, men invented lenses, which are what we call these magic pieces of glass!'

.So, Chris thought, men had been using glass for years to help them to see better.

Then he heard Miss Mackirk say, 'And Chris has been given some bits of magic glass, too. When he's looking through them he can see things better than he's ever seen them before. Let's have a look at them, Chris.'

Chris got his glasses out and put them on. The boys and girls leaned forward. They had laughed at his glasses. Now Chris was smiling. Nobody else in his class had magic glass to look at the world through, and many of them wished they had. Wasn't he lucky?

Our mothers

Project outline

Near Mothering Sunday in the spring the children will be reminded in shops, on television and radio, of their mothers, and how to show their love and appreciation for them. Although many of the reminders will be of a commercial nature, none the less they will be there and, particularly when working towards an assembly, the teacher will want to follow them up.

Probably some children in the class have baby brothers and sisters, or their mothers are awaiting the birth of a new baby. It would be helpful if an expectant mother could come to talk to the class about the preparations she is making for her baby, eg hospital or clinic visits, clothes, pram, etc. If a mother comes with her baby she could talk about the ways in which she looks after him. She should be asked to make sure that the love and security that surrounds him is emphasised. The children should be led to realise that these things were done for them, too, and that, long before they were born, their mothers loved and cared for them.

What does Mother look like? From mothers in general, each individual mother should now be considered. Subsequent drawings or paintings should show this individuality — no two mothers are exactly alike. Perhaps older children could write a poem, or describe Mother's looks in writing. Any writing or artwork should be kept.

Mother's household jobs should be talked about. The children could make a miming and guessing game of these. In many homes today, the mother does her normal household work and manages to cope with a full or part-time job as well. A block graph could show numbers; some children will know what work Mother does, and will be able to write or draw about it. Drawings and writings entitled 'What my mother does for me' should be kept.

Living in a family can never be all take, and the giving is very important if the family is to be a happy one. Talk with the children about the times when Mother herself could do with help, and ask for their suggestions for giving that help. A class picture of 'Mother needing help' should be made to show at the assembly.

Now the children should think of the little acts of love shown by nearly every mother to her child. The child may not even by conscious of these; they may have become so much part of the mother-child relationship that reminders of them need to be given; the arms ready to pick up and hug, the get-better or good-night kiss, the hand to be held, the story in bed, and so on. The children should list things, act them, draw them happening, or write a prayer of thanks for them.

Next, talk about what mothers would like best as a present, and what the children would most like to give her if money was not limited. Presents such as a diamond ring, a new motor car, a gold dress, are only dreams at present, and the children will realise this. What they can give her now will cost nothing — their love and thoughtfulness. Any writing they do should begin and end in the same way: 'If I had enough money I would give my mother ... but instead I will give her my love and help.'

The thinking of the preparation period should now be clarified for presentation at the assembly.

If the children's individual drawings and writings have been done on uniform-size paper, they should now be gathered into a decorated card for giving to Mother on Mothering Sunday.

The assembly

Hymns and songs

When we are happy, full of fun	NCS 29	
Father, we thank you for the night	NCS 32	SSL 1
At half past three we go home to tea	NCS 43	SSL 58
Mummy does the shopping	NCS 95	

Poem

My mother's love

I didn't want a bath last night
But Mummy said I should,
I grumbled and was very slow,
And wasn't very good.

I said, 'The water's much too hot',
I said, 'The soap's got lost';
(I'd really broken it in half
To make my Mummy cross).

I put the flannel up the taps,
I tipped up the shampoo,
I used my sister's bubble bath
And talcum powder too.

When Mum came in she was quite cross,
And I was very glad,
I wanted her to be upset
And look a little sad;

It served her right for saying
I'd got to go to bed.
She dried me without speaking;
She only shook her head.

I hurried into bed last night,
I didn't want a book,
I didn't want a good-night kiss,
I didn't want to look.

'Good-night, my love,' my Mummy said,
'And don't be sad for long,
However much you don't like me,
I love you all along.

I love you just like breathing,
It goes on night and day,
And when you wake tomorrow
You'll feel better right away!'

Prayer

Lord Jesus, hear our thankfulness,
And with your love our mothers bless;
May we love them as we should,
And show our love by being good.

Stories

Bible stories: Samuel's mother, Hannah — 1 Samuel 1.1-2, 9-12, 19-28
Jesus in the temple — Luke 2.41-52
Caroline's present (told in full)

76

Caroline's present

One day Caroline's mother bought her a present. It wasn't her birthday, and it wasn't near Christmas, and she hadn't been particularly good — not that she could remember, anyway. The present was wrapped up in brown paper and Caroline felt it all over. There was a soft lump in the middle, and what felt like long, thin sticks pointing out at each end.

'Aren't you going to open it?' asked Mother.

Caroline tore the wrapping paper away. She pulled out a ball of beautiful blue knitting wool, and a pair of silver knitting needles. 'But I can't knit!' she said.

'It's time you learnt,' said Mother. 'I'll show you how to do it after tea.'

Mother had to cast on the stitches for her, just twelve to begin with while she was learning. And then she taught her what to do, how to put the needle into the front of a stitch, put the wool round, and pull the needle through the loop. It was very slow at first, and it was difficult to remember what to do next, but gradually the knitting grew, first one row, and then the next.

'What shall I make?' Caroline asked her mother. 'Shall I make a jumper?'

'You need a lot more practice yet,' said Mother, smiling. 'And you haven't got enough wool for that. Why not make a scarf for your doll?'

Caroline wished she'd thought of that herself. Her doll would look nice in a blue scarf. Then all of a sudden she had a much better idea. The wool had been a surprise present from Mother — perhaps she could make a surprise present for Mother with the wool! In two weeks' time it would be Mothering Sunday, and she could give it to her then. Should she knit Mother a scarf? There wasn't enough wool. Perhaps a hair ribbon would be better — Mother had such lovely long fair hair, and a blue ribbon would make it even lovelier. Caroline looked at her twelve stitches and at the few rows that she had knitted. If she did some every day it would be just the right length for a ribbon in two weeks' time. Only now she would have to keep it a secret, and that would be difficult. Mother allowed her to read in bed for fifteen minutes every night; now she would have to spend that time knitting, and put it away when she heard her mother coming to say goodnight.

So every night Caroline knitted in secret until the ribbon became quite long. She counted the stitches quite often. Some nights there were twelve but sometimes there were only ten. She could never understand where they went to, but she added a few more. One night she had fifteen, so she dropped three off the end to make it the right number. She noticed, too, that the wool she had already knitted wasn't quite as bright a blue as the wool still left on the ball. Some of it was even a dirty grey colour. She wondered how it had changed. There were a few holes, too, but they looked rather pretty. It would

77

be a lacy ribbon. At last it was quite long. Caroline asked Grandma to finish it off for her because she knew it couldn't be quite right just to pull the needles out and leave it like that.

The day before Mothering Sunday Caroline wrapped the blue ribbon in pretty paper and wrote a little note. It said, 'For Mummy — because I love you, from Caroline.' She hid it under the bed.

Next morning, very early, she went downstairs and found Daddy getting Mother a cup of tea. He had put a lovely red flower on the tray next to the cup. 'Is that because you love Mummy too?' asked Caroline as she skipped up the stairs in front of him.

Mother was already sitting up in bed, looking very beautiful, with her fair hair loose on her shoulders. Caroline hugged her and gave her the present. Mother looked surprised and pleased as she opened it.

'It's a hair ribbon — I knitted it for you all by myself!' said Caroline. Mother seemed so happy with her present. She held it up and said it looked beautiful. Caroline loved Mother so much; she was pleased she had made her own present for her, even if it did look a bit dirty and the sides went in and out, not really like a real ribbon.

And Mother loved Caroline so much that she wore the grey-blue ribbon all day, even when they went to church that morning. 'It's the best present I've had for a long time,' she said.

Palm Sunday

Project outline

The teacher preparing herself and her class for this assembly will want to concentrate on the joyfulness of the occasion rather than on the impending disaster that the entry into Jerusalem heralded. Jesus, the one who had gone about the countryside doing good was, as he entered the Holy City, recognised by the common people as a king and a hero.

Perhaps this assembly will be one of the last before the Easter holidays, and it is unlikely that the teacher will have much time to spend preparing it. This project, therefore, is full of stories rather than activities although some suggestions for these are included. It is a good thing, especially at this time of year, for the children to come to a closer understanding of the kind of man that Jesus was. And when they have come to know him better, it is a natural thing for them to want to share him, and the joy and excitement of Palm Sunday, with the rest of the school.

For at least four days before the assembly, the teacher should select stories of Jesus meeting the ordinary people of Palestine and building up relationships with them. These stories could be told in a straightforward way to the class, or read to the boys and girls from Bible story books. How much more effective they will be, however, if the children become part of the story; and how much better will they come to know this remarkable man, this healer, teacher, friend, if they feel personally involved, as if they have really met him. And this can be done. One story told in this way is given here in full, and is designed specially as part of a series of stories which the teacher will be able to construct herself in the same manner from the biblical passages given. She should endeavour to project the children straight into the story, with the use of 'we' and 'us'. She should be able to take them with her, not simply point the way, through the 'frame' into the storyland beyond.

Class story (based on Mark 1.16-20)

Meeting Jesus

Shall we go down to the beach today? The beach in Palestine, very near where Jesus lives. The sun is very hot in the market-place where we've been playing, and it would be nice to paddle in the cool water. There are Mark and

Hannah; let's ask them to come too. Down the stony, narrow little street, our feet hot and dusty, past the white stone houses, until we come to the lake. It shines like glass, as smooth as a mirror. We go past the wooden fishing boats on the pebbly beach — straight into the water! It's cold and fresh. Mark has gone right in and is rolling over and over where the water is shallow. If we stand on this rock we can look down at the pool beneath us. We can see the pebbles at the bottom, shining blue and gold — and there's a tiny fish! Perhaps one day we could go out in one of those big brown fishing boats with Simon and Andrew the fishermen — go a long way out into the lake, where the water's deep, and we'd look down to where it's dark and blue. We might see great shoals of fish caught in the big nets. Usually they fish at night, but sometimes, early in the morning, we can see them pulling in the nets, heavy with silver fish.

There's Simon now, standing in the shallow water using a casting-net. If we go closer we can watch him; perhaps he'll catch some fish. Hannah is a little afraid of Simon; he's so tall and strong and sometimes a little gruff. But Andrew, Simon's brother, and their friends John and James are both there today, so let's go and sit near them.

John sees us first. 'Hello, come and sit here, it's much cooler,' he says. He's mending some holes in his fishing net. So we all squeeze into the shade beside the boat. Simon doesn't say much today, but John starts telling us about a man called Jesus. A carpenter, he used to be, from Nazareth. He's left there now, and visits other towns and villages, teaching and talking to the people. John says he talks about the kingdom of God. Simon says he's heard that Jesus needs a little band of friends to go with him. It's lonely on some of those roads across the hills, and sometimes Jesus needs strong men to help when there are crowds of people trying to see him.

'Would you go, Simon?' we ask.

'Can't leave my fishing,' says Simon. 'I've got to look after my boat and the nets, and I must sell the fish we catch. Besides, this man Jesus wants clever friends, not fishermen like us!'

'There's someone coming down from the hills,' says Hannah, looking up. We all watch as the man strides down the hill and jumps on to the pebbly beach. We can hear the scrunch of his sandals on the stones as he comes towards us. Simon leaps up. 'It's Jesus!' he says. 'What does he want here?'

The men smile a welcome, and Simon tries to rub his hands clean on his tunic. We just stand and watch, looking at Jesus' face and not taking our eyes away. He is a young man with kind eyes, and a broad smile, which is meant for us, too. He puts a hand on Simon's shoulder in greeting, such strong hands, hands that have used hammer and saw. He talks for a few

80

moments with Simon and Andrew and James and John, smiles at us again, and then begins to walk away over the stones to the village. Then he stops and looks back. Simon and the others are still standing where they were, watching him. Suddenly Jesus calls, 'Follow me!'

Simon drops the net he is holding. 'I will follow him,' he says. 'Wherever he goes, I will go. Whatever he does, I will be there to help. He can count on me!' He follows John, who is already walking up the beach with Andrew and James, following Jesus.

'Follow me!' What magic words they were! He just said them to Simon and the others, and they went to him, like pins being drawn to a magnet. What a pity we're not big enough to go ourselves, to share his adventures, to stand up for him, or just listen to him talking. He'd got a gentle voice ...

' "Follow me!" he said,' says Mark. 'Come on then, let's go!' And we all race up the beach and out on to the dusty road. But we don't know which way they went — up to the hills where Jesus came from, or on through the village?

'Never mind,' says Hannah. 'Tommorrow we'll look until we find him, and then we'll see how far we can follow him.'

Other suggestions for similarly treated stories:
    Serving Jesus — Luke 9.10-17
    Loving Jesus — Matthew 19.13-15
    Watching Jesus — Luke 5.17-26

The assembly

If the teacher feels able to continue this style of story-telling to the whole school for the assembly, she should certainly do so. However, many will feel that a shorter, simpler, and less personal approach would be more fitting. It will be very helpful, though, to talk to the school about the week's experiences-through-stories. Tell the children about the kind of man the class discovered, not just an account of the incidents in his life that were told. There may be children's illustrations to show; and writing done, and read aloud by the children, of their impressions of Jesus.

If possible, organise a simple Palm Sunday procession. The children of the class responsible for the assembly should enter after the main school, each child carrying a 'palm branch' (bracken makes an excellent substitute). Joyful music, singing, or a percussion band should accompany this, while some children, or the rest of the school, shout 'Hosanna!' Good, clear pictures of the life of Christ should be displayed, eg *Jesus Pictures* by Frances Hook (NCEC), or *New Testament Pictures for Today* (Church Information Office).

Stories

Any as suggested in the project outline; also
Jesus the King — Luke 19.28-40 (told here shortly and simply)

Jesus the King

'Nothing exciting ever happens to me!' thought Reuben, as he walked along the village street. Then he heard shouting and saw people running. 'What's going on?' he called.

'It's Jesus, coming this way!' a boy shouted.

Jesus, the teacher, was on his way to Jerusalem! 'Wait for me!' called Reuben.

A large crowd was waiting for Jesus. 'Can you see him yet?' someone asked.

'There he is!' a small boy shouted. 'He's on a donkey, and he's coming this way.'

Reuben climbed a tree to get a better look. One of the branches broke away. 'I can use this to wave,' he thought.

Other boys tore down branches too. 'Let's welcome Jesus like a king!' they said.

People cheered Jesus, and men threw down their coats for the donkey to walk on. 'Hurrah!' they shouted. 'Here comes King Jesus!'

Reuben had never seen the people so happy. Perhaps Jesus would ride straight into Jerusalem and turn out the Romans! But he didn't look like a warrior — just kind, and happy, and friendly. His was the sort of face to make everybody glad, and Reuben wanted to love him for ever.

Hymns and songs

Jesus comes	NCS 67
The children were praising	NCS 68
Hurray for Jesus	SSL 50
We have a king who rides a donkey	SSL 51

Poem

Shout hurrah!

Shout hurrah when Jesus comes
Riding down the hill,

82

Wave your arms and stamp your feet
To show him how you feel.
Wave the green palm branches,
Jesus is your king;
He loves to see you dancing,
He smiles to hear you sing.
Shout 'Jesus is forever!'
Follow him always,
And with your happy voices
Fill all the world with praise!

Music
    Procession of Palms, Williamson

Prayer
    We are happy that we know you, Jesus. We are happy that we can follow
you. We would like other people to know about you, too.

Easter

Project outline

Many teachers find it difficult to present Easter to young children, yet it is the most joyous of all Christian festivals. Probably one of the difficulties lies in the fact that the spring term usually ends before Good Friday, and often before Palm Sunday. Is it best then to ignore Easter altogether? If so, how is it best to cope with Good Friday? Can the children comprehend the love that conquered death? For many Christians the words, 'Jesus died, but rose again' are never separated, and this is what the teacher should seek to teach.

As at Christmas, end-of-term activities may make a comprehensive project non-viable. The teacher should simply make it her task to create a joyful mood, concentrating on the risen Christ. If the crucifixion story is told, it should be followed quickly with the story of the resurrection. If Jesus the man, the friend of little children, has been sympathetically and lovingly presented, then the shock of his death, with nothing to follow, will be too much emotionally for the children. They will be able to experience real relief and happiness in knowing that Jesus died — but is alive.

One approach which may be followed is to help the children to think of good things coming after bad, new out of old, joy after disappointment, and happiness after sorrow. This may seem too mature a theme to give young children, but even the youngest has seen the sun come after rain, morning after night, and re-creation after hard work. With these simple analogies they will be able to see Easter as it is. The story for this assembly should come first, and be followed by a short, simply told version of the Easter story.

If the teacher is preparing the assembly with her class in the days before-hand, the children should be given the opportunity to become familiar with the life story of the butterfly (or the tadpole or dragon-fly, already suggested in the *Spring* assembly). Pictures, picture-strip stories, models and collections could be made along with creative writings on the subject.

The assembly

In the Easter holidays

Grandma was coming to stay with Vicki and Darren for the Easter holidays. Mummy said that they must all think of interesting places for her to see. They would be able to go all together in the car.

'I think she would like to see the wishing well,' said Vicki. She had once been there and wished. She couldn't remember now whether her wish had come true, but it had been a lovely day.

'And we must go to the lighthouse,' said Darren. Daddy had taken them right to the top last summer, and Darren wanted to have another look at how the huge pieces of glass worked.

But when Grandma came she said there was one thing she wanted to see more than anything else. It was the butterfly farm a few miles away. 'Such beautiful butterflies,' she said; and so it was arranged.

Vicki wanted to see the butterflies, too; she had heard about them from her schoolteacher. The butterfly farm had two big greenhouses full of bushes and plants. All the summer the butterflies flew round them, wild and free and colourful, resting here and there on a leaf or flower.

But it was early spring, and still quite cold, when Vicki and Darren went with Grandma.

'There's not a lot to see at the moment,' said the man as he took their money at the gate.

Inside the greenhouse it was warmer, and Vicki looked for the fluttering butterflies. Miss Jeffs had said that there were peacock butterflies, red admirals, and some rarer swallowtails. Vicki couldn't see them. Grandma pointed to a bush.

'Look, Vicki,' she said. Vicki saw some nasty brown shapes, rather like curled up dead leaves, hanging from some of the twigs. She turned away; she wanted to see a butterfly. 'Look again, Vicki,' said Grandma. Darren heard her as well, and he came over to where Grandma pointed. One of the things that looked like a dead leaf was wiggling.

Vicki squeaked. 'What is it?' she asked.

'Just you watch for a few minutes,' Grandma said.

The dead leaf stopped quite still. Then suddenly it looked as if it were going to break — it had split open. Vicki and Darren saw what looked like a crumpled piece of damp rag struggling out. It clung to the split case with six pin-like legs, and within minutes had stretched itself into a butterfly shape. It flattened its wings; Vicki and Darren saw that they were yellow, cleaner and brighter than they had ever seen before.

'It's beautiful!' they whispered, not wanted to disturb it. It seemed impossible that something so beautiful could have come out of that ugly dead shape on the twig.

But it had happened! They knew, because they had seen it with their own eyes.

Jesus visits his friends

Jesus' friends were sad. Only a few days before, Jesus had ridden happily into Jerusalem on a donkey, and everyone had cheered and shouted. Then he had been taken away and killed by some people who hated him.

Jesus' friends thought they would never see him again. They stayed close together in a house in Jerusalem, talking about the things Jesus had done, and remembering the stories he had told. They were very sad.

And then, on Sunday evening, something exciting happened. It was so exciting that it was hard to believe! Suddenly, Jesus was with them. There he was, in the room! His friends could hardly believe their eyes. How happy they were; their sadness was forgotten. Jesus was with them again.

But one of Jesus' friends was not with the others when they saw Jesus. His name was Thomas. When he heard that the others had seen Jesus, he did not believe it. 'I won't believe it unless I see him myself,' he said.

A whole week went by. Jesus' friends did not see him again, but they were happy, because they knew Jesus was alive again. All except Thomas; he was not happy. 'I don't believe it!' he said.

The next Sunday evening the friends were in the house again, talking together about Jesus. This time Thomas was there, too. Suddenly, Jesus was with them. There he was in the room! Jesus turned to Thomas, 'Here I am, Thomas,' he said.

And Thomas was happy, too. He had seen Jesus with his own eyes. Now he believed that Jesus was alive again.

Hymns and songs

Seeds and bulbs are all asleep	NCS 16
At Easter time the lilies fair	NCS 69
When Easter to the dark world came	NCS 70
In the early morning	SSL 49

Poem

Wake up!

'Wake up!' said the crocus,
'Wake up!' said the sun,
'You've been asleep all winter,
Now springtime has begun.'
Buds and bees and baby birds
Wake up in the sun,
And little lambs are playing
Now springtime has begun.
Jesus lives at Easter,
The world awakes in spring,
And everyone is happy
To welcome him as King!

Music
Russian Easter festival overture, Rimsky-Korsakov
(Use the closing section)

Prayer (with response said by the children)
For flowers that come from bulbs and seeds,
We thank you, Father God.
For baby animals in farms and fields,
We thank you, Father God.
For mother birds feeding their young,
We thank you, Father God.
For the sun that comes after the rain, and for happy things that happen
after disappointments,
We thank you, Father God.

Being brave

Project outline

Here is an assembly that needs little more than a day's preparation. It could therefore be used, as is suggested in this book, at the beginning of a term, when teachers and children are preoccupied with settling into school routine once more. If it is used at the beginning of the summer term, it could easily be linked to St George's Day, which falls on April 23. The story of St George has long fascinated children of all ages, and fighting a dragon is the ultimate in bravery! The story of St George could be substituted for the presentation of bravery as set down here — which is a rather free, yet controlled, dramatic story. If there is time, and the teacher feels so inclined, a whole project can be built up around the topic of being brave. Pictures of knights in armour, models of castles, soldiers, princes, giants, and even ancient biblical heroes, could be included.

But to the teacher with a dramatic gift, and a certain ability to tell stories, the notes given here will present a challenge which she may wish to try out. It would probably be an advantage if she could equip herself, with or without the knowledge of her class children, with a few items which could be used as props. These could include a sword, a princess' head-dress or long skirt, an ogre's mask, and a two-metre-long sheet of paper cut as battlements of a castle. None of these things is really necessary, but they would add to the dramatic content of the story as it unfolds.

Unfolding is perhaps the keyword to the whole presentation, as we shall see.

The assembly

The subject of being brave is one which is probably connected, in the minds of Infant children, with fairy stories: the bravery of the prince fighting his way through the undergrowth to rescue the sleeping princess; or the brave little tailor and the giants. This assembly is designed to touch first upon this common interest, and then to bring the subject of bravery right down to the level of the children's own situations.

The first part of the assembly will need to be presented as intimately as possible, with the children sitting on the ground as near as possible to the seated teacher. Although she herself will need to anticipate some of the suggestions likely to be made by the children, she must also be able to let the story take one or two unexpected turns, and to steer it, rather as she would steer a car. She should also have with her some small envelopes: three with the words *Knight, Soldier,* and *Prince* written inside, three with the words *Castle, Palace*, and *Edge of the world* inside, and three with the words *Giant, Monster, Ogre* in them. She should then launch the do-it-yourself story in this kind of way:

'We're going to make up a story. I haven't got it written down, because I want *you* to tell me what will happen in it. But I do know what I want it to be about — someone being very brave. What sort of people are brave? ... Yes, soldiers, ... and ...' (Use suggestions from the children.)

'Some of those people are written in these envelopes. We'll open one to see who is going to be brave in our story.' (Let a child select one envelope from the first group of three; open it and find out the subject of the story.) 'What is it? A knight ... what do knights wear? Yes, armour, silver and shining ... where does this knight live? Let's find out by opening another envelope.' (Same procedure as before, using second group of envelopes.) '... in a castle. Now, also in this castle there lives a ...' (choosing from the last group of three envelopes.) '... giant. Now, this knight wants to marry a beautiful princess, but where do you think she is?' (Get suggestions and use them as the story proceeds.) 'What do you think the knight can do? How can he prove he is fit to marry her? Who does he have to fight ... or do a brave deed for ... etc.'

Let the story go on in this way until it seems to have come to a satisfactory conclusion with the knight showing his bravery and conquering the giant and winning the fair lady! Never mind how conventional and predictable it seems. The children will love the idea of building the story, and will probably insist that it goes along usual fairy tale lines. Conclude with words such as these:

'All these things happened a long time ago. I wonder what people have to do today to be brave?' And the teacher could then launch straight into the story of a little boy's bravery (given later in full): *The courage of Adrian.*

Hymns and songs

When we are happy, full of fun	NCS 29
When a knight won his spurs	SSL 34
Look out for loneliness	SSL 36
Think, think on these things	SSL 38

Bravery

Sometimes you can see bravery,
Like when a man
Pulls a small boy out of the road
To save him from a car.
Or on television
In a film about battles
When the soldiers go forward
To fight and perhaps be wounded.
Or you can hear it —
Hear being brave,
When a boy in the park shouts
'I'm not afraid, I'll climb that tree!'
or 'fight that boy',
or 'play that trick'.
    But sometimes bravery doesn't show.
    You get a feeling, right inside,
    You feel screwed up,
    Afraid and
    Frightened.
    Being brave is when you face it,
    Whatever you're afraid of.
    It's when you say, 'I'll do it',
    Or 'I'll go', or 'I don't mind'.
If you've never been brave
You won't know what I mean.
But if you have
You'll smile and feel warm,
— And you'll be ready
To be brave again.

Music
    Opening movement from *The three Elizabeths,* Coates

Prayer
    O God, we often want to be brave and to do really daring things. Help us to see that being brave doesn't always show. We know that, whatever happens, you will be with us.

Stories
   Bible stories: David and Goliath — 1 Samuel 17.4-11, 32-37, 48-50
                  Paul's shipwreck — Acts 27.27-44
The courage of Adrian (told in full)

The courage of Adrian

Mrs Walker's class of boys and girls was excited. It was their turn to lead the assembly for the whole school on Thursday, and they knew exactly what they had to do. They had all been talking about being brave. Susan's father was a fireman, and he had come to tell them how all firemen needed to be brave every time they answered a call. John's uncle was a policeman, and John told the class about the time when his uncle had had to arrest some dangerous criminals. And George's grandfather had let him bring to school a medal which had been presented to him for bravery when he was a soldier. Susan and John and George had all written a few sentences about what Father, Uncle Robert, and Grandad had done, and lots of children had painted pictures of big red fire engines and people being rescued by the firemen. Then Mrs Walker asked the boys and girls in her class to imagine they were doing something brave, and to draw pictures of it.

Michael drew himself rescuing another boy from a ledge on a mountain. Donna saw herself as a nurse, saving the life of an old man who had been in an accident, and Joanne was jumping into a swimming pool to save her friend from drowning. Adrian had drawn himself fighting a very much bigger boy in order to defend his baby brother. Mrs Walker smiled to herself. She couldn't imagine Adrian ever doing anything as brave as that. He was a very quiet boy who was a little afraid of the bigger boys at school. He didn't really like any of the rough games his own friends played; he didn't really have many friends at all. But his drawing was very good; one of the best.

Mrs Walker said that a few of the children could hold up their drawings at the assembly service, and then tell the rest of the school what they were about. She chose Michael's and Paul's — their pictures were so big and clear that Mrs Walker knew those at the back of the hall would be able to see them easily — and Penny's, which was about a girl rescuing a dog from a very deep pit, and Adrian's. They all looked pleased when she told them — all except Adrian. Mrs Walker looked at him. He was sitting very still and had gone as white as a sheet.

'And you can tell the boys and girls about your pictures,' Mrs Walker was saying. 'You will have to use your loudest, clearest voices, and speak — nice — and — slowly. We'll have a practice tomorrow.'

'I don't want to,' said Adrian.

91

'Oh, come on, Adrian,' said Mrs Walker, 'You've done a lovely drawing. Everyone will want to know what it's about.'

The next morning before school Mrs Walker found Adrian's mother waiting to speak to her. 'He didn't go to sleep for ages last night,' she said, 'and he didn't want to come to school today. He says he's got to say something in the assembly.'

'Well, yes,' said Mrs Walker. 'But if he's too upset perhaps he needn't do it. I'll have a word with him.'

And she did.

That morning, before the other classes met in the hall for assembly, Mrs Walker took her class in for a practice. Those who were to hold pictures up sat near to her. Adrian was still there with his picture, sitting very close to her.

'I don't think Adrian will say anything,' Susan whispered to John.

'He's too frightened; perhaps he'll cry,' said John, and they giggled.

Mrs Walker had heard, though, and she looked sharply at them. Then she bent to whisper something in Adrian's ear.

When the assembly began Mrs Walker talked to the school about being brave, and then, one by one, the children sitting by her read their stories and showed their pictures and talked about how brave they would like to be.

When it was Adrian's turn, Susan and John and the others stared at him and waited for him to burst into tears. But Adrian, with his back held stiff and his face white with fear, stood there and told the school how he thought he would like to fight big bully boys who made him frightened and unhappy in the playground. When he had finished, he sat down quickly, and his face had gone all pink.

'These boys and girls have been telling you about their dreams of being brave,' said Mrs Walker, 'but one of them, Adrian, has done something just a little better — he has actually *been* very brave, here in front of you all. He has conquered his fear. Adrian didn't want to sit up here in front of the school, and then stand up and speak to everybody. But he was brave enough to do it. We can't often rescue people, or save them from drowning, or fight bully boys, but often we need to be brave — like Adrian has been — in quite another way.'

And the boys and girls in the hall seemed to understand at last what bravery was all about.

'Good old Adrian,' whispered John.

Saying 'Thank you'

Project outline

Sometimes taking things for granted is very common among young children. The teacher is often sadly aware of this as they snatch proffered toys, the morning milk, or the many items distributed daily in the class-room. Watching a line of children take their lunch plates without a 'thank you' is another common reason for the teacher to be disturbed. In many schools, though, good manners are insisted upon, and the boys and girls are pulled up sharply when they forget a 'please' or a 'thank you'. But even in such schools an assembly emphasising the need for saying 'thank you' — to each other as well as to God — will not be out of place.

A fairly recent school outing, or a film show or other school entertainment, or a visit by the road-safety expert, or even the routine inspection by the school dentist or nurse, can be used as an introduction to this particular topic. The children in the class, after talking about this visitor, or the outing, should then be encouraged to write 'thank you' letters to the person or people concerned. If this is not possible, then a corporate letter of thanks could be devised using the children's suggestions. Their own illustrations should be included in the letter. The teacher will then be able to begin the actual assembly service by telling the rest of the school about this act of thanks.

Saying 'thank you' at school should be thought about next in the class-room: 'thank you' to each other, to the teachers, to the dinner ladies, and to the caretaker. Perhaps a group of children could be delegated to count the number of 'thank you's' said by themselves to others, or by others to them, or both, in a given period of time. The dinner staff, or the caretaker, or the school secretary, would be surprised and pleased to receive a posy of flowers, letters, or pictures, as a 'thank you' from the children for the work that they do in the school.

It should be suggested, too, that the children notice the times when 'thank you' is said at home, and reminders given of the need for constant awareness of when thanks should be given.

How often service and help go unnoticed and unacknowledged! Now is the time to direct the children's thoughts to the need for saying 'thank you' to God for all his loving-kindness. A large display panel could be assembled for each of the 'thank you to God' subjects that are suggested for this assembly. First, thanks for his gift to the children of parents, brothers and sisters, and home. Pictures, either cut from magazines or drawn by the children of their own houses and families, could be displayed as a montage, with the title *Thank you, God, for our families and homes*. Similar panels could be made for two more subjects: God's living things — animals, birds, trees, flowers etc; and the food God gives us. Try to vary the method of display for each of these, eg the food could be shown as empty packets and tins. If a grace is said at school lunch time, this could be talked about as a way of saying 'thank you' to God, and perhaps a new one could be composed by the children.

All this work and thinking should then be shown and described to the school at the assembly.

The assembly

Hymns and songs

First the seed	NCS 24
We thank you, loving Father	NCS 31
Think of a world without any flowers	SSL 15
The flowers that grow in the garden	SSL 53

Poem

Thank you

'What do you say? ...
I think they're Mummy's favourite words —
'What do you say?'
 ... When I've been given a sweet,
or an ice,
or a toy.
 ... Or when my coat's been done up,
or my shoes,
or my hair.
'Now, what do you say?'
 ... When I've been out to tea,
or the park,
or the sea.
Well, what do I say?
    Thank you!

94

For having fun, and having friends,
>Thank you, God.

For mothers and fathers and happy homes,
>Thank you, God.

For eyes and ears and voices,
to see and hear your world, and to praise you,
>Thank you, God.

Stories
Bible stories: Jesus gives thanks — John 6.5-13
>The leper who said 'thank you' — Luke 17.11-19

John's thanks (told in full)

John's thanks

'I'm going to bed early tonight,' said John.

The last time he'd said that he had had a bad cold. 'Are you ill?' asked his mother.

'What's the matter?' asked his father.

'You must be stupid!' said his big sister Alison.

I wonder if you can guess why John wanted to go to bed early? No, he wasn't ill, and he hadn't broken anything, and he wasn't even very tired! It was his birthday the next day — and he wanted to be up early enough to play with his presents before he went to school!

Next morning he certainly woke much earlier than usual, the house was still dark and quiet. John lay in bed thinking. Today he was eight, as old as his friend Malcolm! And after school Malcolm and two more boys were coming to his house to tea. Mother had promised to make it a special tea, with baked beans and chips.

'Come on, everyone! Wake up!' John couldn't keep quiet any longer, and he bounced into his parents' bedroom. 'It's my birthday!' he announced for anyone who wasn't quite sure about it. He knew there was a really smashing present waiting for him from Mummy and Daddy. He knew all about it because he had specially asked for it, and had even been with Daddy to choose it last week. It was a cricket bat! A beautiful, pale, clean, smooth cricket bat!

'Ooh, thank you!' he said, and hugged his mother and father. Alison came in then with a parcel. John liked the wrapping paper, because it had boats on it, but he was too excited to think of trying to save it as he tore open the parcel. Inside was a brand new pencil case. He unzipped it and found some new pencils and a rubber inside. 'Thank you, Alison,' he said.

Grandma, who lived only three houses up the street, called in before he went to school. She gave him a red cricket ball. 'I thought it would go with your cricket bat,' she said.

'Oh yes! Thank you, Grandma,' said John.

Just before going to school, John opened the door to the postman. He had brought him three more parcels, a letter from Auntie Pauline with a postal order in with it, and lots of birthday cards.

'Thank you, postman,' said John.

On his way to school he met his cousin Tommy. 'I've got a present for you at home,' Tommy said. 'You'll have to come round on the way home tonight.'

So many presents! And even when he got to school, the class all wished him a happy birthday, and his teacher gave him a sweet.

After school that day, John and his three friends called first at Tommy's house, where he was given a model car. 'Coo, thank you!' said John, as he ran it along the carpet. Then he and his friends ran home. Each of them gave John a little present, and they all thought the tea that Mummy had prepared was smashing.

'Thanks for getting it all ready, Mum,' said John.

And then, suddenly, it was bed-time again.

'Oh, no!' said John in surprise. 'My birthday's gone much too quickly! I'm sure it was a much shorter day than yesterday.'

'But you've still got all those presents,' said Mummy. 'For a long while they will remind you of how happy your birthday was.'

John had had a lot of parcels and cards and letters by post from friends and relatives who lived too far away to see him. 'You'll have to write "thank you" letters to them,' said his mother.

John wasn't very keen on this part of birthdays. It was easy to say 'thank you', but a bother to write it! But Mummy insisted that he should, and that he should begin doing it the very next day. 'Saying "thank you" to people you can't see is important,' she said. 'How will they know you're pleased otherwise?'

When John climbed into bed that night he said one more 'thank you'. 'Thank you, God,' he said, 'for a lovely day. It's been wonderful!'

That was an important 'thank you'; he couldn't see God, but he wanted God to know he was happy.

Milk

Project outline

The daily drink of milk is something that most children in the Infant school look forward to. The teacher can make a most successful short project round this bottle of milk, and an assembly should lead easily and spontaneously from it.

'Where does milk come from?' the teacher asks at the beginning of such a topic. And we cannot assume that all young children will know. 'The milkman' will probably be an immediate answer, and the children will have to be led back, in imagination, and through pictures, to the farm. Plenty of pictures of cows, calves, milking sheds, milking machines and churns should be available, together with publicity material and information sheets from local dairies or the Milk Marketing Board. Many of the older children will enjoy discovering from books and leaflets about the pasteurising and bottling processes. It may be possible for some classes to arrange to visit a dairy farm or milk-processing or bottling factory. Such a visit could be talked about, recorded and illustrated, possibly in the form of a frieze. Templates of cows are usually available in Infant schools, which the children can draw round and colour or cut out. The best pictures, however, will come from real observation of cows or, if this is not possible, from photographs or good illustrations. There is nothing to better a six-year-old's large square cow, painted thickly with powder or tempera paint, with its four legs indiscriminately positioned, and the large pink fingers of the udder dangling from some central point! Very young children will enjoy fashioning cows from modelling clay and making cereal-box sheds.

Even the youngest child will be able to contribute to a discussion on the different forms of milk known to them, and what milk can be used for. Many will have baby brothers or sisters and will appreciate that milk is, or was, a vital part of their diet. Encourage them to bring cartons that have contained milk powder, or labels from tins that have held evaporated or condensed milk. The boys and girls will have watched milk being used in cooking; they could probably write or talk about this. Pictures from magazines should be cut out and made into a montage, showing such things as custard, cream on fruit, blancmange, sauces and so on. Some children may not realise that milk can be eaten — in the form of butter, cheese, yoghurt or ice-cream. Cartons and wrappings from all these products, and others that will come to mind, should be collected. They can be used to furnish a dairy or farm shop in the class-room, providing practice in number work.

Practical work in the class-room could include making butter: a very simple process. Half fill a screw-top jar with milk (the richer and creamier the better), and pass this from child to child, shaking it constantly. Gradually, as this is done, the fats will solidify. The liquid can then be strained off, and salt added to the butter that is left in the jar. If there are any facilities for cooking at the school, the children would enjoy making scones, using milk to mix with the flour, fat and small amount of sugar. The butter they have made could then be sampled on their home-made scones! With careful forethought the teacher should be able to save a few of these scones and some butter to show to the school at the assembly.

The thoughts of the boys and girls in the class, and subsequently those taking part in the assembly, should now be directed towards children in other countries. Reminders of the babies known to them and photographs of well-fed and thriving babies (remember to include some of coloured children) in our own communities should be shown. Through the media and the posters of various caring agencies, some boys and girls will have heard about deprived children in the third world. To others it will come as a surprise that not every child has enough to eat every day; that they have no homes as we know them, and rarely enough clothes to wear, Perhaps the seeds of wanting to care and share will be planted in some of the children from this assembly.

The assembly

Hymns and songs

We thank you, loving Father	NCS 31
For all the strength we have	SSL 16
Kum ba yah, my Lord, kum ba yah	SSL 23
When I needed a neighbour	SSL 35

Poem

For what we have ...

The cow was big and beautiful,
Her coat like creamy silk,
Her eyes were large and deepest brown:
I thanked God for her milk.

98

The hen fussed in the farmyard
    Scratching with her legs,
Her feathers smooth, her darting eyes:
    I thanked God for her eggs.

The cornfield waved so golden,
    'It's ripe,' the farmer said;
I watched the cutters cutting:
    And thanked God for my bread.

When I was feeling thirsty
    I went to the kitchen sink,
I turned the tap with my fingers:
    And thanked God for my drink.

I have enough to live on,
    I've even a bit to spare —
I thought of the starving children,
    And asked God to help me share.

Prayer

Thank you, God, for the milk we drink, the food we eat, and the clothes we wear. We thank you that in this country there is enough for everyone. Help us to find ways of sharing what we have with people in other countries.

Stories

Bible story: The caring Lord: Healing the nobleman's son — John 4.46-53
Nikki's gift (told in full)

Nikki's gift

Nikki Ekeledo stood in the middle of the pavement. His eyes were fixed on a big poster on the opposite side of the road, right under the railway arch. He couldn't read the words, but he hardly noticed them, because he was so busy looking at the picture. The little boy in it was about as big as Nikki, and he had skin the same colour as Nikki's, 'Like a lovely piece of plain chocolate,' as his nice next-door neighbour always said. Nikki couldn't see the boy's face for he was walking away in the picture, and he was carrying a bit of wood as a walking stick.

But what Nikki was really staring at, with his little black eyes almost popping out of his head, was the little boy's bottom. He had such a big hole in his trousers that his bottom showed right through! Nikki looked down at his own smart trousers. Father had only bought them for him on Saturday; they were new and clean and they fitted him perfectly. He thought of his other clothes, his tee-shirt with the bright pictures on it; and his football shoes and his new trainers. They were lovely to wear, but he couldn't do the laces up yet. His Grandma Ekeledo was going to give him a red track suit for his birthday, too.

Nikki looked again at the black boy in the poster. He was very clever, really. He seemed to be walking quite fast, yet he was balancing a heavy bundle of old rags on his head. Whatever did he want those for? And under one arm he was carrying a rather dirty old blanket. Nikki tried to read the words underneath, but they were too difficult.

'Nikki!' He heard his name, and turned round. His sister Peghi was coming along the path, swinging her shoe bag and her cardigan. 'I'll race you home,' she said.

But Nikki didn't move. 'Look at him!' he said, pointing to the little boy in the poster. 'Why hasn't he got a proper pair of trousers? You can see his bottom!'

Peghi stood and read the words on the poster. 'He hasn't got anywhere to live,' she said. 'He probably hasn't got anything to eat, either.'

Nikki had noticed that his legs looked awfully thin.

'Christian Aid is asking for people to send money to places like Africa and India,' Peghi added. 'A lot of African and Indian children are starving and have no homes,'

'I'm African, and I'm not starving,' said Nikki, 'and I've got proper clothes. Why aren't I starving?'

'Because Father's got a good job and is paid enough money to buy us food and clothes and a house,' said Peghi. She thought of the good tea her mother would have ready for them. 'Come on,' she said, 'I'll race you home!'

When they sat down to tea that night their mother brought them huge platefuls of hot stew and vegetables. It was Nikki's favourite meal. He asked for a glass of milk to drink; it was cool and fresh. He thought of the little boy on the poster. He wished he could send him some of the stew, and a pint of milk; he would love it. Nikki hadn't realised before that there were little boys who looked just like him (little girls, too, he supposed), who just hadn't got enough to eat, or to wear, and who hadn't got houses to live in.

Just then Father came in from work. 'Want to earn some money, Nikki?' he asked. 'You can bring all those books in from the car, then sweep out the car with a dustpan and brush.'

Nikki didn't mind jobs like that. Of course, he didn't always get paid for doing them, but this time he could do with the money, he wanted to buy one of the new ice-creams from the shop down the road. The job was finished in about twenty minutes, and Father gave him a bright shiny coin. Nikki thought of the boy in the poster again: he lived in Africa, and Father said it was always hot in Africa. That boy would just love an ice-cream! But Nikki was old enough, and sensible enough, to know that he couldn't send him an ice-cream just like that. It would melt before it left the post-box. Nikki grinned to think of the ice-cream being squeezed into the envelope and then through the narrow opening in the letter-box. He thought of it oozing out all over the other letters and postcards and packages. Wouldn't the postman get sticky fingers when he opened the box to put the letters in his sack! No, he definitely couldn't post an ice-cream to Africa!

And then he saw the little boy again, the African boy with his bottom showing. This time his photograph was on a leaflet on the hall table, along with a small white envelope.

'What does it say?' he asked his mother as she came past.

'Christian Aid,' she said. 'They're asking for money to help people in other countries — people who haven't enough to eat, or enough to wear, or anywhere to live. I expect Father will put something in the envelope.'

'I wanted to buy the little boy an ice-cream,' said Nikki. 'He's the same colour as us. He hasn't got proper clothes, and he looks hot and hungry.'

His mother said, 'You can't give an ice-cream, can you? But what were you going to buy the ice-cream with?'

Nikki looked at the shiny coin in his hand. 'But they have different money in Africa. Father told me that once. He wouldn't be able to use it there.'

His mother explained that a lot of the money given to Christian Aid would go to paying men and women to teach the people in Africa to become better farmers and fishermen. It would help to buy tractors and fertilisers for them to use. It would help to buy building materials for houses, and it would go towards clothes and mattresses. Nikki thought he understood. He slipped his money into the tiny envelope and looked again at the photograph of the little African boy. 'I hope you get some new trousers soon,' he said.

Looking for signs

Project outline

Signs, symbols and signals are all around us, and are generally recognisable and easily understood. In the period of preparation for the assembly the teacher should look for signs in the local environment. She will need to be able either to point them out to the children in her class in a 'walk about', or to reproduce them in some form for class-room use. Road signs are probably the best starting point; the children know that these signs bear messages that the public can understand and observe. The boys and girls may have to cross roads at traffic lights, or watch a crossing warden hold up a 'lollipop' sign for motorists to see and obey. Older children would enjoy a quiz, questionnaire, or workcards on the recognition and interpretation of these signs. Patterns of circles, triangles and rectangles using road signs as a basis for designs could be made, and 'play roads' can stretch across the class-room or playground where the 'traffic' can be checked with home-made road signs. If the school is conveniently situated, similar work could be done with ships' signs, lights and flags and lighthouse beams, all things which convey messages to people.

Analyse these messages with the children: some messages warn, some inform, some direct. Talk with them about the use of colour: red for danger or stop — traffic lights, fire engines, car braking lights etc. Often yellow and black are warning colours in animals and insects, eg the wasp, tiger. Animals have their warning signs as well as humans: the dog's bark, the lion's roar, the rabbit's tail, and many others. Reference books should be searched through for further information.

Not all signs are visual; some can be recognised only by sound, eg the fire drill bell or buzzer at school. Encourage the children to think of more: the ambulance's siren (clear the way), radio time-pips (information), clapping at a concert (approval), front door bell or knocker (announcement), or the bus bell (message to the driver). Perhaps these sound signs could be copied or mimed by the children for the rest of the class to recognise, an activity that could be adapted for the assembly.

We look for signs often, and recognise them in the coming of the seasons, in threatened storms, or 'red sky at night'; in a raised body temperature or rash, both signs of illness, and in a baby's cry, a sure sign of distress.

As the assembly draws near, mention the signs humans give each other. What signs tell a child that his mother is pleased or angry? How does she show it? Her whole body is full of messages: the way she stands, her hands, her tone of voice, her words, her smile, her frown. The children should record these signs, in pictures, words, or masks and mime. Facial expressions hold many messages, and think of hand and finger messages and signs too; the children will be able to suggest several. 'How do you greet someone across the street?' (with a wave), 'How can you ask someone to come to you without saying a word?' (beckon them); 'How do you know which way to run to find a lost ball?' (someone points). Practise conveying these and other messages by sign language.

An attractive display of work done on this project should be made to show the rest of the school, sound should be reproduced for a guessing item, and facial messages conveyed. The extent to which we depend on signs of one kind or another will surprise many, and this can be linked for the assembly to the signs of a living God, clear and recognisable to the receptive and perceptive person.

The assembly

Hymns and songs

Look up! Look up!	NCS 1
Here we stand on the pavement	NCS 37
This is a lovely world	SSL 8
I'm very glad of God	SSL 22

Action poem

I can move my head, just watch it go,
A nod for 'Yes' and a shake for 'No'. (Nod and shake)
If I screw up my eyes I can look quite sad,
But look at my smile when I'm feeling glad. (Frown and smile)
Hands can be signs as well, you see,
If I do this it means 'Come to me'. (Beckon)
When my arm goes right up, the answer I know, (Raise arm)
When I point with my finger it often means 'Go'. (Point)
When I see you I wave, I clap when you're good, (Wave and clap)
And when I do this, be quiet as you should. (Finger to lips)
When my hands are together I keep them there,
That means I talk to God in prayer. (Praying hands)

Prayer
Dear Father God, may what I do, and what I look like, make other people happy every day.

Stories
Bible stories: The sign of the rainbow — Genesis 9.8-17
The sign of a friend (David and Jonathan) — 1 Samuel 20.1-3, 17-42
Signs of God (told in full)

Signs of God

Every night Andrew lay in his bed watching while Mother put his clean clothes ready for the next morning. The she bent down to kiss him, 'Goodnight, God bless,' she said. Every night it was the same, and Andrew liked it that way. It made it easy to snuggle down afterwards and fall asleep quickly.

'What does "God bless" mean?' Andrew asked when his mother said it one night. 'It means "May God take care of you and love you",' she replied.

Next morning Andrew woke quite early, but it was already light and the birds were singing. 'Good morning, God bless,' he said to them. His teddy sat on the end of the bed; 'Good morning, God bless,' said Andrew.

He looked at his books until Father came in. 'Good morning, Andrew,' said Father. 'Good morning, God bless,' said Andrew.

'Where is God?' Andrew asked Mother after breakfast. She thought for a moment and then said, 'God is all around us, like the air we breathe.'

'Then why can't I see him?' asked Andrew.

'When we go out today we'll try to find him,' Mother promised.

On their way to the shops Mother pointed to something on the grass. 'Look,' she said. 'There's a daisy.' Andrew bent to look at the little white flower. 'That's our first sign of God,' said Mother.

Andrew heard a bird singing. 'Is that God, too?' he asked.

'It's one of God's signs,' said Mother. 'It's a reminder of him.'

Then they saw a girl helping to pull an old lady's heavy shopping trolley.

'That's another of God's signs,' said Mother. 'We often see him in the kind things people do for one another, and in their happy faces.'

Andrew saw a lady walking with two sticks; she was trying to open her garden gate. Andrew ran and opened the gate for her.

'I've just seen God again,' said Mother. 'He's right inside you, too, Andrew, and I'm so happy.'

Andrew was happy too. God's signs were everywhere. Now he had some idea of where God was, and what he was like.

Rules

Project outline

Children in Infant schools already know a great deal about rules. In this project we will examine some of the rules we follow and find out why they have been made. By question and answer find out from the children what rules they are expected to observe at home. These will vary from family to family, although the children may be surprised to find that many of the rules are common to most families. Older children can write about these rules, and all can draw them being obeyed or broken. A discussion about why these rules at home have been made should follow. Most of them, it will be discovered, are for the safety or comfort of the whole family.

Three large illustrated posters should be made for display: the first showing rules at home, using the drawings and writings already prepared; the second, rules at school; and the third, rules of the road.

When beginning to talk about school rules, make use of any new ones that have been made recently, or old ones that have been re-stressed in the past few weeks. Again examine the reasons for having these rules; they are nearly all for the safety and comfort of the school community. With writings, drawings and paintings, and copies of the instructional notices around the school, produce the second large display panel.

Lastly, think together about the rules that they, as children, are expected to keep in the street, eg the pedestrian code, and also parental and commonsense rules about playing in the street, holding hands to cross a busy road, and so on. Road signs giving warnings or instructions to pedestrians or drivers of vehicles should be studied and understood. Any in the vicinity of the school could be visited and drawn, with written explanations of what they mean; these should be used on the third large display panel.

A large plan, or relief model, of the school neighbourhood could be made and the local street signs reproduced upon it. Discuss with the children what would happen if these signs were ignored and the rules broken. Again emphasise that rules often keep people safe. Further work on policemen, traffic wardens, or crossing patrol men or women could be done, and the results shared with the whole school at the assembly.

The assembly

Poem

Rules

Go to bed, it's six o'clock,
  And please don't tease the cat;
Wipe your feet when you come in,
  And don't slide on the mat.

Come to school at nine o'clock,
  Go home at half past three,
And when the whistle blows at play
  Stand still as you can be.

Look right, look left, look right again,
  Then, if the road is clear,
You walk, not run, to get across —
  You watch, you think, you hear.

So many rules I must obey,
  I often wonder why;
I'm told they're not to catch me out,
  But to live safely by.

Prayer

Jesus followed rules. He was taught, 'Love God, and love the people you meet every day.' Help us to follow the same rules as Jesus did, and to love you always, dear Father God, and the people we meet.

Stories

Bible stories: In the time of Jesus there were many rules regarding what could and could not be done on the Sabbath day. Jesus believed that people were far more important than rules and the gospels give many instances of the way in which he broke rules in order to serve people, eg,

The crippled man at the pool of Bethesda — John 5.1-10
The man with dropsy — Luke 14.1-6
(See also Matthew 12.1-8, 9-14; Luke 13.10-17)
Janet breaks a rule (told in full)

Janet breaks a rule

'What are you doing in that cupboard, Janet?' Mother called. She was doing the washing-up in the kitchen, but she had heard Janet climbing up to the medicine cabinet. 'Don't touch those pills,' Mother warned.

'Oh Mummy!' said Janet, 'I must have some pills — I want to play hospitals with my dolls. I'm not going to put them in my mouth or anything!'

Janet's grandmother had given her a nurse's outfit to wear. There was a blue-and-white striped dress, a white apron, and a little white cap. And one of those upside-down watches that nurses wear pinned to their aprons. Janet had put her two dolls, Amanda-Jane and Christobel, in her doll's cot, and her teddy bear lay on a cushion. Really, Christobel didn't look at all well today. She was pale and lay with her eyes shut tight. She needed one of Mother's headache pills, Janet thought.

'You mustn't touch those pills,' Mother was saying. 'Shut the cupboard door and go away and play.'

'Oh, all right, then,' said Janet.

Mother still had her back turned. Janet had a small jar of pills in her hand and she slid quickly out of the door. 'Mummy won't notice I've got these,' she thought. 'She won't miss them for half an hour.' She looked at the pills carefully when she got back to her dolls. 'What's so special about them, anyway?' she thought. 'They're only for headaches!'

She pushed one of the pills down Amanda-Jane's little open mouth. Christobel was still sleeping; besides, her mouth didn't open. She put the pills on the floor beside the doll's cot. 'You can take another when you wake up,' she said to Amanda-Jane. Just then Mother called from the kitchen.

'Barry's woken up, Janet,' she said. 'Can you play with him while I finish getting lunch?' Barry was Janet's little brother. He was only just over a year old. He couldn't walk yet, but he crawled everywhere on his hands and knees.

'Oh, all right!' Janet said. 'But he's not to touch my dolls.' Barry often spoiled her games. Mother said he was too young to understand what he was doing.

Janet looked at him as he crawled quickly towards her. 'Stay over there!' she said. 'Don't you come near my dolls.'

Barry crawled away and sat examining something by the bookcase. He was very good and didn't bother her for quite a time. Janet looked at him again. He was sitting quietly, putting something into his mouth — sweets? No! Janet sat up, suddenly frightened. Barry was picking little white pills off the floor and looking carefully at each one. Had he put any in his mouth?

'Mummy!' shrieked Janet. 'Come here!'

As Mother came into the room she could see what was happening and rushed to Barry. 'Have you eaten any?' she asked him, picking him up. But Barry just smiled.

Mother called the doctor and Barry had to go to the hospital to have lots of tests. But he was lucky — he seemed to have just licked one pill. It had had such a horrid taste he had spat it out on to the carpet.

'Now do you understand the rule about never touching the pills or taking anything out of the medicine cabinet?' Mummy asked Janet.

Janet had been badly frightened, and she understood. The rule had been made and had to be kept so that everyone in the house would be safe.

'I'll make sure I keep the rules next time,' she said.

Friends

Project outline

For this project the teacher needs first to look at the children in her care; to be aware of any rifts that there may be, and any long-standing friendships. Is the class on the whole a happy one? Do any of the children stand out as dominating characters and, if so, can they dominate for the good of the other children or not? Are there any lonely children who seem to have no friends? Are there any who seem to repel all friendly advances?

Next the teacher needs to think about the purpose of working towards an assembly on 'friends'. Can she bring the children to understand what makes a good friend, and how friends can make the whole of life fuller and more meaningful? Can she expect them to consider a little more the feelings and needs of others?

Friendships at school should be the main theme. Spend a little time encouraging the children to sit next to their friends in class — and note the popular pupils, the ones many boys or girls would sit next to if given the choice. What makes this or that child popular: is it always personality? Let them choose, within certain limits, what they would like to do with their friends. Talk afterwards about why they chose to do particular things: were they both good at it, or interested in it? Did one choose and the other acquiesce? At this point the children should write about their best friend at school. They could discover more about this friend by answering questions suggested by the teacher, eg 'What is your best friend's favourite colour?'

After a playtime, get the children to try to recall all they did: the games they played, other friends who joined them. They should talk about this together, or write about it. A large picture should then be built up of drawn, coloured and cut-out pictures of a playtime, showing the current favourite games: skipping, ball, hopscotch and so on.

Use some activities that the class as a whole can try, suggesting that the circle of friends could be much wider than they generally believe. If there are one or two 'unpopular' children in the class, try to create friendships between them, suggesting games or activities they would enjoy together. Help the others to understand the plight of lonely boys or girls, and get them to think of ways of drawing them into the circle of friendship.

Other ideas on friendship will occur to the teacher who has time to take the topic further: friends at home, for instance, those met after school has finished. How is the time spent with those friends? Are they invited to each other's houses? The children might enjoy planning a tea-party, either in words or a series of pictures, showing the food and games that would be enjoyed by them both.

Thinking along these lines, the children will probably be able to help the teacher plan their own assembly.

The assembly

Hymns and songs

When Jesus was a little boy	NCS 57
Let's beat a song of praise	NCS 71
We hurry to school in all kinds of weather	NCS 77 verse 2
The ink is black, the page is white	SSL 39

Poem

James and I

James and I
Are friends;
We play and work
And work and play,
   Till schooltime ends.

James and I
Go out,
We roll and run
And walk and slide,
   And love to shout.

James and I
Like planes
And trucks and bikes
And cars and vans,
   We play good games.

James and I
Eat food
Like fish and chips
And beans on toast,
   They all taste good.

Friends for now,
Good friends;
We'll laugh and cry
Will James and I,
   Till friendship ends.

Prayer

O God, our loving Father, thank you for the happiness we can have with friends, and for the fun of laughing and playing together.

Stories

Bible stories: The king's son and the shepherd boy — 1 Samuel 17.58;
            18.1-4; 19.1-7
                The good Samaritan — Luke 10.25-37
    Katy's friends (told in full)

Katy's friends

Katy had two good friends at school — Jane and Paula. When she ran into the playground every morning they were always there waiting for her. They showed each other their treasures and shared each other's secrets. When the whistle went they lined up together, ready to go into the class-room. They sat at the same table, and were on the same reading books.

One day a new girl came. She had just moved into the town with her family, and her mother had brought her to the school. Their teacher, Mrs Davis, looked at the spare chair at the table where Katy and Paula and Jane sat.

'Sit down there, Susan,' said Mrs Davis, pointing to the chair. 'Katy will look after you today.'

Katy looked at Susan. She had ginger hair. Katy didn't like ginger hair. She moved a little further away. Susan wasn't much good at anything either. She didn't know many of her sounds, and she could only just write her name. Katy had been able to do that for months. And Katy's reading book was one of the most difficult in the class. Katy looked at Susan.

'Can you read?' she asked. She already knew the answer, and she laughed nastily when Susan said, 'No.'

'Can you do number work?' Katy asked.

'What's that?' said Susan, and Katy laughed again. She giggled with Jane and Paula, and they didn't talk to Susan again for ages.

'Katy, don't forget to look after Susan in the playground,' said Mrs Davis when they had drunk their milk. Katy was cross. She always played with Jane and Paula, just the three of them. But she knew that Mrs Davis would be cross if she didn't take Susan's hand as they lined up and went into the playground. She saw Mrs Davis watching from the window.

As soon as Mrs Davis had gone away to have her coffee, Katy ran off to find Paula and Jane. 'Where's Susan?' they asked.

'Oh, I left her by the wall,' said Katy, laughing. 'She'll be all right. We'll go back for her later.'

But they forgot. Susan, with her back to the wall, watched as the children raced round, shouting and laughing. There were so many of them, and some of them were very big. No one took any notice of her. When the whistle went

Ben

111

all the children ran into lines to go to their classes. Susan looked for Katy, but couldn't see her. She joined the children in a line near her. 'You're not in our class!' they said. Susan began to cry.

'What's the matter, Susan?' said a voice near her. It was Mrs Davis who had come to fetch her class in. 'Are you lost?' she asked, and took Susan's hand. 'We'll go and find the others.'

In the class-room again, Mrs Davis was very cross with Katy. 'I thought you would look after Susan and be her friend,' she said.

Katy glared at Susan. How silly of her to have got lost! And Mrs Davis thought that it was all Katy's fault. Mrs Davis was giving out sheets of coloured paper and the scissors. Katy didn't like cutting out very much. She could never get the scissors to cut properly.

'Put your name on the paper,' said Mrs Davis. Katy could do that easily.

Susan wrote half of her name, and then stopped. 'What do I put now?' she asked Katy, in a whisper. Katy just laughed, and turned to speak to Jane.

Mrs Davis showed the children how to fold the paper, and then told them to make little cuts along the folds. She did one to show them. When she unfolded the paper, there was the prettiest little paper mat that Katy had ever seen. 'Now you make one,' she told the boys and girls.

Jane and Paula were soon snipping away. Katy's scissors slid along the paper. They wouldn't cut, not even make a mark. Perhaps they were a blunt pair. She changed them with Susan's, while Susan was still folding the paper. But Susan's were no better. She wished she could cut out like Jane and Paula. Suddenly she heard a voice beside her.

'Shall I do it for you?' said Susan.

'You?' said Katy. 'You can't even write your name!'

'But I can cut out!' said Susan, and showed Katy how to hold the scissors more easily. She made a few snips along the edge of Katy's folded paper; they were straight and clean. Katy looked at Susan. 'Thanks,' she said, and smiled.

Katy practised holding the scissors, while Susan helped. At last she had cut a few small notches. It wasn't as difficult as she had thought. But she could not have done it without Susan's help. 'Thanks,' she said again.

Funny, how Susan had helped her, even though Katy hadn't done much to make friends with her. She was truly sorry about that, and later she asked Susan to sit next to her at dinner. After that there were always four friends together in the playground, Katy, Jane, Paula and Susan.

Surprises

Project outline

It is often assumed that young children love surprises, and this may be true in part. But how they cling to an established routine, a well-known story, or a favourite old toy! Perhaps this is because their lives are full of surprises, of new things encountered, of new experiences; and the familiar gives a sense of security in an otherwise bewildering world. This is particularly true after the child first begins school.

Begin the project by providing surprises for the class, not all in one short session, but spread over a day. A visitor might arrive to talk to the children, or a small animal be introduced into the class-room, or a biscuit be given to each child with his morning milk. It might be possible to arrange with a colleague to change class-rooms for a session. Anything that makes a change from the normal routine, and happens suddenly, will provide the surprise.

At the end of the day talk about the surprises and the ways in which the children reacted to them. Did they enjoy them? The following day pursue the subject, with a toy like a Jack-in-the-box. Talk about the element of surprise when they play 'Beep-bo' with younger brothers or sisters, or when an older person plays a trick on them. Some children will enjoy playing tricks on the rest of the class. Given a free rein, these will not all be pleasant surprises, but they will provide the teacher with an opportunity to point out that there are often unpleasant ones, too. Ask the children to write or talk or draw about times when they have received an unpleasant surprise. (Often Infants are badly shocked by the school's fire alarm.)

Later talk about planning surprises, providing much fun to the giver and the recipient. The class should plan a surprise for the assembly; one or two of the children's suggestions for this may be feasible. The teacher should also have ready one or two ideas that can be talked over and worked out. Giving small buttonhole posies to the head teacher or staff could be considered; or a short play or mime could be presented, or musical instruments played to accompany the hymn or song. The teacher and class taking the assembly might sit in different positions in the hall, necessitating those that listen facing a new way.

At the assembly the teacher should tell the school about the surprises that have been going on in the class-room during the preparation period. Pictures and writings should be displayed or read out, and the suprises that have been meted out to the school commented on. She can then go on to talk about God's surprises — hidden landscapes suddenly revealed by a break in the hills, a burst of unexpected bird song, a sudden movement in the grass, a dart of colour in a pond, a chick breaking out of an egg, or the glory of a white world discovered after a night of snowfall. Each new day brings surprises to be encountered with joy or met with fortitude.

The assembly

Hymns and songs

Skipping down the pavement wide	NCS 36
I love to think that Jesus saw	NCS 59
Come and let us sing	NCS 78
To God who makes all lovely things	SSL 9

Poem

Surprises

I had a surprise last springtime,
I went to the woods one day,
I saw lots of beautiful bluebells,
    Looking so bright and gay.

I had a surprise last summer,
Walking along the sand,
I found a crab, a baby crab,
    And I held it in my hand.

I had a surprise last autumn,
A great big knobbly ball
Fell, with a conker inside it,
    Down from the chestnut tall.

I had a surprise last winter,
The world was all shining white,
The snow had covered the garden,
    Silently during the night.

Praise God for lovely surprises,
He gives us all through the year,
Thank you for eyes to see them,
And memories to hold them dear.

Music
La boîte à joujoux (*Children's ballet*), Debussy
(1   The box of toys;   4   After fortunate times)
Slow movement from *Symphony No 94* (*Surprise*), Haydn
(Play the excerpt in which a loud stroke on the drum sounds in the middle
of a quiet passage)

Prayer
Use the last verse of the poem above

Stories
Bible stories: Joshua takes Jericho, simplified from Joshua 6.1-16,20
           Paul's shipwreck and discovery of an island, from Acts 27
Patrick's surprise (told in full)

Patrick's surprise

Mummy was busy washing up. 'Come and play,' said Patrick, who was only
four and too small for school.

'Oh Patrick,' said Mummy. 'I've got far too much to do. Grandma's
coming today, and I've got to get her room ready when I've washed up.'

'Why?' asked Patrick, who was always asking questions. Of course, he
really understood that Grandma would need clean sheets on her bed, and
flowers on her table, and that all the rooms should be clean and tidy.

'It would be a nasty surprise if Grandma came and found all your toys on
the floor,' said Mummy. 'I saw your tractor on the stairs this morning. She
might fall over it if you don't put it away.'

Patrick liked surprises. He couldn't really understand how a surprise could
be nasty. 'Can we go to the shops?' he asked.

'No,' said Mummy, firmly. 'I did all the shopping yesterday. Besides, it's
raining.'

Patrick went to the window. The rain poured down all over the garden. It
was grey, and looked cold. Patrick was surprised; he hadn't expected to see
the rain. It was rather a nasty surprise. 'Can I paint?' asked Patrick.

'No,' said Mummy again. Patrick wondered why. It was such fun to get out
the paints. Once he had painted a picture of a house. It had been a big

115

house, and he had had to paint some of it on the table because it wouldn't all fit on to the paper. And then he had painted his fingers and put a big dab of red paint on the dog. It had been a surprise to Mummy, and she hadn't been very pleased; he supposed that had been a nasty surprise.

He crept under the kitchen table. Sometimes he pretended that it was a house. Sometimes it was a cave. Today it looked just like a table. He sat beside the big plastic basket that Mummy kept for the clothes that needed ironing. It was empty at the moment, except for a big red towel. Then Patrick had an idea; he would give Mummy a surprise, a really nasty surprise, worse than the paint or the rain or Grandma falling down the stairs.

Mummy was still busy at the sink. She was peeling vegetables ready for tonight's supper. If he turned into a monster he could come out all growling and she would have a surprise: a bad surprise. She would run away like Little Miss Muffet. He turned the clothes basket upside down and put the big red towel all over it. And then, very quietly, he lifted up one side and crawled underneath. It was just the right size to cover him up completely.

Patrick crept out from under the table. He growled, a long, ferocious growl, a monster growl. Mummy turned round. The clothes basket and the big red towel moved forward, growling.

'Help!' said Mummy, when she saw it. 'I won't stay here with that horrible monster!' She ran into the dining room. The monster followed, very slowly, because he couldn't really see where he was going. He peeped out from under the basket. Mummy stood on a chair by the table. He wondered how he could get her now. If he stood up the clothes basket would fall off his back, and she would know he was inside. He bumped into a chair.

'Ouch!' he said, as the basket scraped his shoulder. And then something awful happened. He was going quite fast across the carpet, when he went straight into a small table. Something crashed down on top of him and bumped the plastic basket so hard that he hit his nose on the floor. He began to cry, and pushed the basket away. Mummy ran over and helped him out.

'Goodness!' she said. 'It's Patrick! What a lovely surprise!' She hugged him tightly. Just at that moment the front door bell rang and they both went to see who it was.

'Hallo,' said Grandma, who was standing there. 'I managed to catch an earlier train. I hope you don't mind me arriving so soon.'

'Another lovely surprise!' said Mummy. She told Grandma all about the monster that had turned into Patrick.

'There's a surprise for you in my case,' said Grandma to Patrick. He was so excited. Really, he thought, nice surprises were much better than nasty ones. And he started to plan one for Grandma.

Disappointments

Project outline

This is an important though rather abstract subject. Disappointment is a feeling that everyone has to cope with, and one's first meeting with it usually comes early in life. Every time a hope is built up only to be dashed, every time an anticipated happening does not occur, there is a feeling of disappointment. This can be a mild irritation when one is twenty-five, or a crushing blow at five years old.

It may be felt that this is only a suitable subject for an assembly or for sharing with a class if some particular event has happened in the school which has left the children with a sense of disappointment.

The teacher should tell or read to the class a story about a disappointment. This could be the one given here, which will be repeated at the school assembly, or a similar one. As she tells the story the children will be stimulated to think of times when they have had to face disappointments. Get them to talk about them; then go on the discuss what happens next — how do they cope? The main reactions will be getting angry, crying, sulking or arguing. Sometimes a kind of detachment occurs, but this is not so common.

What reactions should the child try to show, rather than those just listed? By question and answer type of discussion the teacher can elicit the best ways of coping with disappointment. Reactions such as anger, sulking or arguing serve no useful purpose, and most children can see the sense of this although few will know how to substitute anything better. The teacher should help by presenting imaginary situations, where the reaction could be changed from crying to cheerfulness, and from anger to acceptance. This is a mature attitude and one which the children will find extremely difficult to cope with, but introducing it can only do good.

The teacher will note, and if the members of the class are mature enough talk over with them, that disappointments are sometimes caused by accidents, and sometimes have to be faced for one's own good. The child, for instance, might have set his heart on spending his pocket money on a pen-knife, but is prevented from buying it for his own safety.

The children may also be helped to realise that adults suffer disappointments, and these disappointments are sometimes caused by the children, even unwittingly. A little extra thought might prevent them.

The assembly should be a time when the teacher tells the school what her particular class has been thinking about and discussing. Some situations should be dramatised for the school showing usual reactions to disappointments, and the reactions that would be better.

The assembly

Hymns and songs

Little bird, I have heard	NCS 12
When we are happy, full of fun	NCS 29
I'm very glad of God	SSL 22
God bless the grass	SSL 27

Poem

A disappointment

I'm having a birthday on Monday week,
I'm going to be seven years old.
I've got a surprise in the wardrobe upstairs,
But I can't even peep, I'm told.

My friends were coming to tea that day,
Mandy, and Robert, and Sue;
But a terrible thing has happened to me,
You'd never believe, but it's true.

I didn't feel well when I went up to bed,
Mum thought I had caught the 'flu;
But it's worse than that, there are spots on my face,
On my arms and my shoulders too.

When the doctor came he examined me,
He said I'd got measles for sure,
I'd have to stay in for a couple of weeks
And not let my friends past the door.

My birthday! My friends! What a terrible time,
I'm so sad that I think I shall cry.
Will my surprise have to wait, do you think?
And how can I make the time fly?

118

    Dear God, sometimes we feel sad and unhappy. Nothing seems to be right.
    Help us to keep cheerful and try to change from being sad to being glad.
    We are sorry if we make other people unhappy.

Stories
    Bible stories: The two sons — Matthew 21.28-31
                     The wedding feast — Matthew 22.1-10
    The soldier shop (told in full)

The soldier shop

Shaun and Michael were brothers — twins, in fact, which meant they were
born on exactly the same day. They were seven.
    They were on holiday with their Nana and Grandpa. Mummy was there
too, but Daddy had gone abroad to work, and couldn't be with them.
    They had both been saving their pocket money, and Grandpa had given
each of them a little extra. The family had stayed with Nana and Grandpa
last year and Shaun and Michael had discovered a most exciting little shop.
It was in a tiny village nearby, down a very steep hill. In the shop sat a little
man with only one arm that worked. The other arm, Shaun noticed, didn't
seem to move at all and he always wore a leather glove on that hand. This
little man, though, did the cleverest things — exactly what Shaun and
Michael would like to do when they were bigger; you couldn't really call it
work at all. Each day he sat at a little table making model soldiers, and he
was always surrounded by paint and glue and mess. He sold his model
soldiers in the shop. Shaun and Michael had saved their pocket money to
spend in his shop. Shaun wanted some soldiers like the ones outside
Buckingham Palace, but Michael preferred ones that looked as though they
were really fighting.
    'What shall we do today?' asked Grandpa on the second day of their
holiday. You can guess what the boys said! But Nana was talking about going
to the village fête that was to be held that day. Grandpa said that, because it
was the day of the fête, the Abbey House would also be open to anyone who
wanted to see round it. It was only open six days in the year, and Mummy
and the children had never seen inside.
    'But we could go to the soldier shop first, I suppose', said Mummy. That
would be all right, thought Shaun and Michael. They didn't want to be
bothered going round an old Abbey House.
    It was ages before everyone was ready. Nana had to make some blackberry
and apple jam first, before the fruit went bad, and Mummy was busy writing

a letter to Daddy. Grandpa had to clean his car. Shaun and Michael sat on the front doorsteps and counted their money again and again.

Just before twelve o'clock dark clouds came overhead, and it started to rain. The boys scuttled indoors. Nana and Grandpa looked a bit worried.

'All those people with their vegetable stalls and home-made cakes!' said Nana. 'They'll have them all ready for the fête; now they'll have to move them indoors to the church hall.'

Grandpa thought of old Mrs Knight and her flowers. 'I had better go and help her move them,' he said.

'I don't suppose many people will bother to go to the fête if it's raining,' said Nana. 'All the visitors will go to the pictures or stay indoors this afternoon.'

'They were trying to raise money for the church,' said Grandpa. 'They'll be so disappointed.'

Shaun and Michael wished they would stop talking about the fête. They wanted to go to the nearby village and buy their soldiers. They had talked for so long about getting them.

'Come on, come on!' they said. 'Can't we go yet?' But Nana and Grandpa were still talking and Mummy was joining in, too.

'I think we ought to go and help them move all their stalls,' said Mummy, looking out again at the weather. The rain was still falling down. 'We can go to the soldier shop another day.'

Go another day! Shaun and Michael stood still and looked at each other. Had they really heard Mother say that? 'But you said we'd go to the soldier shop first!' said Shaun.

'Well, I'm sorry, boys, but the soldier shop will still be there tomorrow,' said Mummy. 'The fête can't be held tomorrow, so we really must go to help the people there. Come along now.'

Shaun went to sit on the front doorstep in the rain. 'It's not fair!' he said, and refused to move, even when Grandpa nearly fell over him as he hurried out with an umbrella. Michael was terribly disappointed too. But he knew it was no good crying or anything like that. That wouldn't make anyone change their minds.

They were both so disappointed that they could have made themselves miserable all the afternoon. But instead, 'I'm going to help,' Michael said to Shaun. 'It might be good fun. And Mrs Smith has made some fudge, she told me. Come on!'

So they went to the fête instead of the soldier shop. And they made themselves and everyone else much happier.

And, as Mummy said, the soldier shop was still there the next day.

Helping each other

Project outline

It is suggested that this assembly should take place near the end of the summer term. At this stage of the school year there will probably be little time for a prolonged and highly-organised project. The end of the summer term in most schools is a time of some confusion, with end-of-term records to be compiled, and parents' evenings or open days, concerts or summer fêtes, to be prepared. Some of the older children feel the need to 'move on', and are excited and probably a little apprehensive about the future. In some schools children in the younger classes are receiving smaller children into their midst, maybe for a single visit, or perhaps on a regular weekly visiting basis, to prepare them for their full-time entry into school life. If this is happening there is a particularly good reason for introducing the subject of helping each other.

A similar topic *People who help us* has been suggested for an assembly earlier in the year. In that one, the children were led to be thankful for the help given them by other, usually adult, members of the community. In this topic they will be shown, and experience, how they themselves receive and give help to others of their own age. However, this does not exclude the adults in their immediate circle — teachers, parents, older brothers and sisters. The emphasis will be on seeing the needs of others and acting upon them.

It is assumed here that there will be four days for the teacher to introduce and work on the subject of helping each other before the actual assembly. No elaborate work-schedules need be introduced, no variance from any end-of-term routine, merely a little thinking ahead, and anticipation of events and circumstances which could be used to advantage.

Day one   A 'help circle' should be introduced, or, if a similar scheme has been working well in the class for some time, it should once again be talked about and discussed. The 'help circle' should be a list of boys and girls to whom others can go for help, eg to Maureen and Anthony for help in tying shoe-laces. Children who would normally be called 'monitors' or 'teacher's helpers' would be on this list which will, of course, be individual to the school, class and pupils. On this first day endeavour to make the children enthusiastic in giving and asking for help.

Day two   As well as continuing to keep the 'help circle' active, and maybe thinking of extra work and workers to be included on it, the children should now be encouraged to work and play together in pairs or small groups. They will then experience help from each other in a further, supportive, way, with a dependence upon each other. They will find that games of ludo or snakes and ladders are difficult, if not impossible, when played alone. And how much fun and how much mutual help there is in working through a mathematical problem, however simple, or a piece of English comprehension, with others.

Day three   Emphasis today should be on the times when help is given to the children by adults, especially within the school setting, but also at home. Discuss the times when what the boy or girl is trying to do becomes so difficult that he or she would have to give up if there were no teacher or other adult near. In some schools a parent is invited into the class-room to give the teacher extra help; if this is so, use the experience to discuss with the children how they benefit. They could talk about and list times at home and at school when they have to ask for help — in tying ties after PE, in spelling a certain word, or riding a bike, slicing bread, or doing up inaccessible zips and buttons. Drawings of this kind of help being given and received should be made.

Day four   Today talk with the children about the way in which help is received, and offered. The teacher has probably witnessed a child receiving help ungraciously, either because the help was not asked for, or because the recipient was entirely thoughtless. The saying of 'Thank you', and the mere allowing help to be given, could be talked about. Every teacher, too, will have experienced the too-helpful child, the one who fusses, who seldom leaves the teacher's side, and who is certain to leap to his feet in a state of almost hysterical enthusiasm when aid is asked for. Point out the virtue of being observant and perceptive, of being aware when help is needed, even when it is not asked for, and of acting upon that awareness.

This should be the general pattern of the project. There may be little to show to the assembly, but perhaps the future attitudes of the children will be influenced by these few days of preparation for it.

The assembly

Hymns and songs

Mummy does the shopping	NCS 95
He gave me eyes so I could see	SSL 19

Hands to work and feet to run	SSL 21
Jesus' hands were kind hands	SSL 33

Poem

I've got these hands

I've got these hands that want to do
All sorts of kind things just for you.
I've got these feet that want to run
And do good deeds for everyone.
I've got these ears that want to hear
When people call out 'Help me, dear'.
I've got these eyes that want to see
When people need some help from me.

Prayer

Thank you, God, for all the help other people give me every day. Show me ways in which I can help them.

Stories

Bible stories: Samuel helps in the temple — 1 Samuel 3.1-19
The helpful little girl — 2 Kings 5.1-14
Amanda helps (told in full)

Amanda helps

'Run away, Amanda,' said Daddy, who was trying to fix a shelf on to the wall. 'If you don't move I can't see if the shelf is straight.'

'It is straight, it is!' said Amanda helpfully, and then bumped her head on the corner of it as she moved. It tipped up in a lop-sided way.

'Out of the way,' ordered Daddy.

Amanda went into the kitchen. 'Shall I put the cream on top of the trifle?' she asked her mother.

'Not yet,' said Mummy. 'The custard's still hot, and the cream will melt. Come back in about an hour.'

Amanda kicked the door as she went. 'I don't know what to do,' she said.

'Go and play with Stephen,' Mummy suggested. Stephen was ten. He was in the garden, busy with some planks of wood.

'What are you doing?' asked Amanda.

'Making a tree house,' said Stephen.

'Can I help?' asked Amanda.

'Don't be silly,' said Stephen. 'You couldn't even lift one of these bits of wood, let alone get it up into the tree!'

Amanda tried to lift one. It wouldn't move.

'Go away,' said Stephen.

'Shall I climb up the tree and put them straight?' suggested Amanda.

'No,' said Stephen.

'Shall I bring you a rug to sit on in your house?' said Amanda.

'I've got one,' said Stephen, pointing to an old cot blanket that Mother had turned out.

Amanda sat on the grass to watch him. 'Shall I get you some string, or some nails, or a hammer?' she suggested.

Stephen was getting quite cross. 'When I need your help, I'll ask for it!' he said.

For a little while Amanda watched him. Then she lay on her tummy and looked at the grass. Why did everyone tell her to go away all the time? Why didn't they want her help? Was she really too little to do anything?

She turned round. Stephen was hauling the planks of wood up to a place in the tree where the branches spread out, forming a natural platform. He had thought of a very clever way to get them there. He had fetched the ladder from their bunk beds and stood it against the tree. This made it easy to get to the platform and pull the planks of wood up from the ground.

Just then, Amanda's little white dog, Snowpot, who had been sitting beside her on the grass, gave a little growl. He sat up, looking at the path at the bottom of the garden.

'It's only the next-door cat,' Amanda told him. But Snowpot had gone shooting off down the garden, barking furiously as he went. He raced past the tree where Stephen was arranging his planks of wood up in the branches. The little bunk-bed ladder fell to the grass. But Stephen was so busy he didn't notice.

'I'm not picking it up!' thought Amanda. 'Stephen said when he needed my help he'd ask for it.' And she sat quite still and wondered what would happen.

Suddenly Stephen turned to climb down the ladder backwards. His foot dangled, trying to find the top rung. Suddenly the thin branch he was holding on to snapped, and he nearly fell. Amanda rushed to the tree.

'Wait,' she said. 'Here's the ladder!' In one quick movement she stood the ladder back against the tree and guided Stephen's foot to the top rung. He wouldn't fall now!

'Thanks!' said Stephen. 'Good thing you were there!'

Amanda was happy. She hadn't had to ask if she could help that time. Perhaps just being there was enough, ready, and with her eyes open!

Holidays and summer

Project outline

By mid-July, interest in the coming holidays will be mounting; parents will be making travel plans, and the end-of-year activities at school will be happening. Many of them include fine weather programmes such as sports afternoons or class outings or playground fêtes. This type of excitement, fresh air and warmth, can be used by the teacher in one of several short projects, suggestions for which are given here.

The sun The sun provides warmth for our pleasure, making most people tanned and healthy. It helps growing things, providing long periods of daylight. Talk with the children about places that are hotter than the United Kingdom, eg the Mediterranean, where many children these days spend their summer holidays; what will grow there that will not grow in this country? Talk about the magnification of the sun's rays by use of glass; and telling the time by the sun. Simple sundials could be made, and the shadow cast by the sun noted at various times of the school day. Explore how the sun affects our lives, eg drying clothes quickly, ripening corn and fruits. In many countries food is dried in the sun for preservation, as it was in Palestine in the time of Jesus. Measure shadows at different times of the day and note when they are longest and shortest. Talk about how the sun can also be a danger at times: when is causes sunburn, or is a means of starting fires in forest and woodland.

How we enjoy ourselves in the summer Let the children say and illustrate what they enjoy doing best on holiday; how they enjoy themselves at home and away. How are preparations made for the holiday? (Packing, booking tickets, making picnic meals for the journey, etc.) How will they get to the holiday resort? (See the next paragraph, which overlaps with this theme.) What things can be collected on holiday? (Shells, tickets, picture postcards etc.) Some of the children could make a holiday diary, or picture notebook, or sketchbook. Games to play in the car, or on the beach, or on a boat, might interest the whole class. Children who can swim could give the rest of the class an idea of what it feels like to swim, and of the movements their arms and legs make. Some will be going to the countryside or to farms; talk about what they can expect to see and hear. Share ideas on what they can notice when visiting towns and cities. Other things to note include favourite food on holiday, and what can be done on wet days.

Transport for the holiday How will members of the class travel? Make graphs of this. Pictures of personal transport and public transport can be made and collected. Encourage the children to look for unusual methods of transport (a) in British holiday resorts (coach and horses, tandem bicycles etc) and (b) in foreign countries (donkeys, sledges etc). On long journeys what provisions are made for the comfort of travellers: food, sleeping arrangements, amusements, etc?

Any of these projects could be enlarged as the teacher adds her own ideas, or the spontaneous suggestions of the children in her class, and each can provide material to be shown at the assembly.

The assembly

Hymns and songs

Happy laughter, jolly games	NCS 61
For happy games all children play	NCS 73
Thank you, God, for lovely sea	NCS 76
Lord, I love to stamp and shout	SSL 5

Poem **Holidays**

> Here we go to the sea again:
> Out of the busy town,
> Leaving our house and our friends back home,
> It's over the hills and down.
> Daddy is driving the car for us,
> And Mummy has brought our tea;
> You couldn't wish for a better time
> Staying beside the sea.

Music

Flight of the bumble bee, Rimsky-Korsakov
Overture Fingal's Cave, Mendelssohn
Knightsbridge March from *London Suite,* Coates

Prayer

When we are happy, help us to make others happy too.
When we feel like singing, may we ask others to share our song.

When we skip and dance, may there be others with us.

And, when we feel like praising you, O God, may we show others how wonderful you are.

Stories

Bible story: The picnic on the seashore — John 21.3-13

The end of the holiday (told in full)

The end of the holiday

Jonathan had looked forward to his holiday for ages. He had packed and re-packed his toys many times; he had taken his black and white rabbit to be looked after by his Auntie Jean; and he had bought a big red kite with his pocket money.

The holiday place was a long way away — it had taken them one evening and all night to get there. Jonathan had slept on the train, and then slept on the boat which took them over the sea to a little island which was quite near France. The holiday itself had been the best he ever remembered, and the sun shone every day. They had done so much in the week. They had been to five different beaches, and they had toured the island in a rickety old bus. They had seen a tiny little church and a small airport and a butterfly farm. They had been to the top of a high cliff and flown his red kite.

Then suddenly it was time to go home. Jonathan was quite surprised; he had thought the holiday would go on for much longer. Mother and Father were packing again, and reminding him to wrap his presents carefully. He had bought one for Auntie Jean, and one for his friend Robert, back at home.

This time, instead of travelling at night, they were spending a whole day getting home, so that Father could have a good sleep before going back to work the next day. They had to be down at the harbour, ready for the boat, at ten o'clock in the morning. Jonathan didn't want to leave the little island. He liked it there. He didn't want his holiday to finish at all.

'Why can't we stay another week?' he asked his mother. 'Father could go home and go back to work, but we could stay here. I don't have to go back to school for ages.'

'But Mrs Helen couldn't have us for another week,' said Mother. 'She's got other visitors arriving as soon as we've gone.'

So Jonathan and his parents had caught the boat back; it was a huge boat, Jonathan thought. He spent a long time looking over the rail watching the island disappear into the distance. He found his mother sitting on a comfortable chair in the inside deck. 'I don't want our holiday to end!' he

127

said. Mother tried to get him to look at a book, or to do a puzzle, or to count the suitcases, but Jonathan just sat still, looking very glum. 'I don't want the holiday to end,' he kept saying.

At last the ship pulled into the quay and the engines stopped. 'Keep with us, Jonathan,' said Father. 'We've got to get on the train for London as soon as we get off the boat.'

Jonathan didn't want to hurry to the train. He thought if only he could go slowly it would make the holiday last a bit longer. There was absolutely nothing to look forward to now. Just the long train journey to London, and then the walk to another platform for the short train journey back to the town where they lived.

'Come along, Jonathan,' called Mother.

'Here's a seat for you, right by the window,' said Father, putting the cases up on to the rack in the carriage. 'Only a few minutes before we start,' he said, looking at his watch.

Jonathan sat all hunched up. The window was a bit too high for him to see anything, anyway. He hung his head and thought of the island. He thought of the sunshine and the swimming and the seaweed. It seemed such a long, long way away, and such a long time ago.

The train made a clanking noise and moved forward. Jonathan knelt on the seat so that he could see what was going on. They were moving slowly along the platform. Jonathan looked ahead, expecting to see lines and lines of railway, where the train could go shooting towards London like a long snake.

'Where are we going?' asked Jonathan, and he sounded a little worried. The train had moved away from the station, and was going along by the side of the sea water which was running inland and turning into a river. Out of the window on the other side of the carriage he could see a house — a very close house. If someone had leant out of the bedroom window he was sure they could have touched the train. And there were more houses! It wasn't like a railway at all. The train was actually going straight up the High Street!

'Look!' Jonathan said to everyone in the carriage. 'Our train's going up the road! There are shops beside us — and people on pavements!'

He couldn't believe what he could see. Men, women and children stood back to let the train along, and it went very slowly, just as a car would on a narrow stretch of road. It was very exciting! What a way to end a holiday! He would tell them all at school — he was sure none of them would have been on a train that went up the middle of the High Street. His holiday had been lovely — but the best bit had been when he had thought it was all over!

128